MRS. HUNTER'S
HAPPY DEATH

MRS. HUNTER'S HAPPY DEATH

LESSONS ON LIVING FROM
PEOPLE PREPARING TO DIE

John Fanestil

DOUBLEDAY
New York   London   Toronto   Sydney   Auckland

PUBLISHED BY DOUBLEDAY
a division of Random House, Inc.

DOUBLEDAY and the portrayal of an anchor with a dolphin are
registered trademarks of Random House, Inc.

In this book I share my experience and my memory of the people
whose stories I tell. Except in a very few instances I have not included
details shared with me in confidence. When I have included these kinds
of details, I have done so only because clarity demanded it, and I have
changed the descriptions of persons so that identification is improbable.
I have not, of course, included anything that was shared with me in the
form of a "confession." Throughout the book I have used real names
only when the subjects of the stories—or the surviving members of their
families—specifically requested that I do so. To family and friends who
may recognize their loved ones in these pages, I apologize for any errors
in biographical fact.

Library of Congress Cataloging-in-Publication Data

Fanestil, John.
   Mrs. Hunter's happy death : lessons on living from people preparing
to die / John Fanestil.—1st ed.
     p. cm.
   Includes bibliographical references.
   (alk. paper)
   I. Death—Religious aspects—Christianity. 2. Hunter, Mary Clulow,
1775–1801—Death and burial. I. Title.
   BT825.F23 2006
   236'.I—dc22

                                       2005049704

ISBN 0-385-51606-I
Copyright © 2006 by John Fanestil
All Rights Reserved

PRINTED IN THE UNITED STATES OF AMERICA

10 9 8 7 6 5 4 3 2 I

First Edition

To my grandmother, Marian Smith . . . for rubbing my back . . .

and the memory of

Harry Smith

and

Carl & Esther Fanestil

CONTENTS

Contents

ACKNOWLEDGMENTS

This book was born from life shared with many communities. My most obvious debt of gratitude is to the people of the United Methodist Churches in Calexico, Westchester, Anaheim, and La Mesa, California. Thank you for accepting me as a pastor, albeit a sometimes distracted one. Please forgive me if, in telling your stories, my memory has sometimes come up short. Please know that my affection has not.

Thanks to Ann Taves of Claremont Graduate University for encouragement and counsel and such superb teaching. Thanks to Bob Edgar and Phil Amerson and Jack Fitzmier of the Claremont School of Theology for encouraging me and for letting me teach without a Ph.D. Thanks to CST's faculty and library staff and students for helping me to work through so many things.

Countless friends and colleagues have put up with me talking ad infinitum (ad absurdum? ad nauseam?) about dying. Special thanks to Preston Price, Martha Rowlett, Sue Farley, and Carolyn Bohler. Early drafts were read by Patricia Farris, David Richardson, Lois McAfee, Ward McAfee, and my wife, Jennifer Leich. Thank you for telling me to keep writing.

Thanks to Wallace Alston and the staff of the Center of Theological Inquiry in Princeton. Special thanks to my colleagues in the western seminar of CTI's Pastor-Theologian Program—I knew all along that we were not just drinking whiskey and blowing smoke.

Thanks to Maria Luisa Segurola for her genealogical work on the Clulow family and for her generous correspondence. Thanks to Peter Forsaith of the Wesley Centre at Oxford Brookes University and to Tim Brinton of Macclesfield's Christ Church for their gracious assistance and most helpful leads. Thanks to Greg Anderson for a fabulous afternoon walk in London.

Thanks to my agent, Lynn Nesbit, and to my editors, Trace Murphy and Becky Cabaza, and to their staffs. Thank you for seeing the connections between dying and living.

Not enough thanks can go to my family. Thank you, sibs, for putting up with me . . . and, thank you, Mom and Dad, for putting me up from time to time! Thank you, Ellen and Jacob, for letting Daddy type on his computer . . . I will always love you. Thank you, Jennifer, for your love and friendship and curiosity, and for sharing the search with me.

MEETING MRS. HUNTER
FOR THE FIRST TIME

Some ways of dying are better than others.

No one ever says, "I want to die alone in a hospital room." Yet this is exactly how a great many people die in our day. As death comes into view most people express the desire to be kept "comfortable." The comfort they are thinking of is physical—they want ample doses of pain medication; they don't want to suffer too much. Most, though, have not lived lives that prepare them for the emotional and spiritual challenges that dying invariably presents.

Of course there are exceptions to this rule. In my work as a pastor I've known many people who lived out their dying days with a spirit of considerable peace. These people accepted death as a part of life, and neither they nor those attending their deaths experienced undue stress or trauma. I've also known people who died what are called "good deaths." Having cultivated close personal relationships across the course of their lives, these people were able to celebrate these relationships as they died. They made amends, forgave those who had wronged them in their life, said good-bye to their families and friends.

And then, every so often, I am privileged to witness someone die with remarkable and uplifting grace, an absolute inspiration to others. Adjectives like "peaceful" and "good" do not adequately describe the deaths of these rare individuals. These people die with their hearts full of love and with their spirits soaring. And in their dying they inspire others to a greater appreciation of all that is good in life.

I remember Claire Robbins, a woman who died singing her favorite hymn and reciting the Lord's Prayer. Her son, Jim, would later say of his mother's death, "it was the most beautiful moment of my life."

And I remember Nancy Martens, whose principal preoccupation in her last weeks of life was seeing to it that her husband learned to cook. Nancy received visitors from her deathbed as if she were serving them cookies and tea—in fact, on one occasion that I witnessed just a few days before her death, she *did* serve cookies and tea, while hosting a group of friends at her home. Nancy died with exactly the same reassurances for others that were characteristic of her in days of full health. "Everything will be just fine," she said over and over to her husband. The last thing her family remembers of her is her smile.

And I remember Barbara Ferry, who was so excited to see the effects her dying was having on her family. Her sons were talking to each other for the first time in years, and one of her grandsons had started to pray with her, something he had never done before. Barbara believed that God was using her dying to accomplish miraculous things in the lives of others, and she clapped her hands in glee as she shared with me her plans for her funeral. It was as if she was planning to host her own birthday party and welcome her one hundred closest friends.

For many years I had been impressed by the faith and spiritual depth of people like Nancy and Claire and Barbara. I had shared their stories in sermons, compared notes about them with colleagues, and taken encouragement from them myself during times of grief and loss. For all those years, though, these people had puzzled me. The popular literature on death and dying is filled with talk of anger and remorse, guilt and forgiveness, acceptance and peace. But nowhere had anyone written about the happiness and holiness I had witnessed in my work with the dying. Versed in today's common wisdom about the end of life, and trained in contemporary methods of counseling, I could not account for the way the Nancys and Claires and Barbaras of the world lived and died.

Then one day, in the basement of a seminary library, I came across the stories of "happy deaths" that were popular in religious magazines in both England and America through the eighteenth and early nineteenth centuries. Happy dying was a ritualized way of dying practiced widely for generations—and in fact for centuries across the history of the Christian church. Rooted in the paradoxically good news of Christ's death on the cross, this ritual encouraged those who practiced it to seek an experience of God's grace—what today we would call a "spiritual high"—enabling them to transcend the pain and suffering and grief that come with death.

Fascinated by the curious idea of a happy death, I decided

to browse some stories—"accounts," they were called—from magazines and newspapers at the turn of the nineteenth century. I decided to sample the accounts from a single year and for no particular reason chose the year 1801.

I found myself especially captivated by an account published in England in the July and August 1801 issues of *The Arminian* magazine. Written by an author who identified himself merely as "J. Wood," it told the story of a young woman he called, quite simply, "Mrs. Hunter," who died in London from an unidentified illness, on January 17, 1801, at the age of twenty-six.

J. Wood's "An Account of Mrs. Hunter's Holy Life and Happy Death" included extensive excerpts from Mrs. Hunter's own journal. Again and again, in passages like these, this young woman described her spiritual posture in preparing for death:

> Glory, honour, and praise be to my compassionate God...The desire of my heart is that I may from this moment prove, by happy experience, that I am thoroughly renewed in all the powers and faculties of my soul...
>
> I feel thankful for the grace which I enjoy: I live by faith, and all my salvation is of God...By obeying his Spirit, I find he leads me on to more light, life and love. Glory to God!

As I read I felt I heard a voice—one that sounded profoundly familiar—ringing down through the ages. I was overwhelmed.

I sat steeping myself in the story of Mrs. Hunter's happy death, and a flood of memories and emotions came rushing over me. I thought of Claire Robbins and Nancy Martens and Barbara Ferry, and a host of others I had seen die inspiring deaths—Lucille Callen and Gregory Randolph and Nora Lopez. I thought of my grandmother, Marian Smith, now ninety-four and profoundly frail. When asked how she is doing at this time in her life, my grandmother commonly answers, "Just wonderful. With God on my side I have everything I want or need."

That day in the library, I found in the language of a bygone generation the same spirit I had witnessed in these extraordinary people. I found their seemingly inexplicable cheerfulness; their complete and utter lack of concern for material things; their ever-deepening devotion to God; their preoccupation and concern for other people at a time in life when any objective analysis would lead to the conclusion that others should be concerned about them.

As I read J. Wood's account of Mrs. Hunter's journey, I found myself caught up in something much larger than myself. I felt drawn into a wider spiritual circle, as if I were visiting at a tribal council of my elders. I felt as if a great-great-great-grandmother had come back to visit with me . . . not from the grave, but from the very edge of life. And from her deathbed Mrs. Hunter was sharing with me the mysteries of life and death.

I sat as if surrounded by Mrs. Hunter and these other remarkable individuals, people whose deaths could truly be described as "happy." I found myself wondering . . .

What is the secret of people who die contented and fulfilled? What makes it possible for them to attain such spiritual heights as they approach their physical demise? What enables them to make death a completion of life, rather than a tragic end? And what can they teach us about life and death, love and loss, grief and spiritual growth?

This book will answer these questions by introducing you to Mary Clulow Hunter and to her spiritual descendants. Convention would have it that the ritual of the happy death simply disappeared across the course of the nineteenth century, as custody of the practices of dying was transferred from religious to medical specialists. But this version of events is altogether too simplistic. The ritual of happy dying has not simply evaporated across two centuries of modernization. It has been transformed, to be sure, but it has not been forgotten altogether. Beneath the radar of medical and even psychiatric professionals, people like Claire Robbins and Nancy Martens and Barbara Ferry are in fact still practicing this historic and uplifting way of death. They deserve to have their stories told, and we—faced with so many choices as we ponder the end of life—need to learn the lessons they have to teach.

In Part One of this book, I will introduce you to the ritual of happy dying by walking you through J. Wood's account of Mrs. Hunter's death, shedding light on the history of this remarkable approach to the end of life. At each step along the way I will share the stories of people I now know to be Mrs. Hunter's spiritual heirs. I will try to tell these people's stories as best I can remember them, to honor them as J. Wood honored Mrs. Hunter. I hope that you will be blessed by them, as I have been so blessed.

Part Two of this book will explore the spiritual practices that are the foundation for a happy death. Presented as ten "lessons on living from people preparing to die," these chapters will show that Mrs. Hunter's preparations for death—prayer, reflection, loving God and neighbor, and so on—have their roots deep in the history of Christianity. I will also share the stories of people I have seen put these lessons into practice in our day. I hope that Part Two of this book will become a companion to you in your own living and dying, as you navigate the waters of life and loss and grief.

I believe the ritual of happy dying, rooted in these historic practices, is ripe for renewal in our generation. With the spread of in-home medical and hospice care, the work of dying is being wrested from medical professionals, and being returned to its rightful place in the institutions of family and home and religious community. This is for the good. Dying is not at its root a medical process. It is a process with profound and obvious physical dimensions, but that is only a part of it. Like other natural processes—birth, giving birth, love, making love—dying is a natural process infused with profound emotional and spiritual dimensions. Mrs. Hunter understood her dying moments to be among the most important moments in her life, and she wanted nothing more than to share them with her family and friends. In her dying she was teaching that the way we die, like the way we live, makes a difference—in our lives and in the lives of others.

That first day in the seminary library, as I reached the conclusion of J. Wood's account, I was taken aback by the sheer exuberance of Mrs. Hunter's happy death:

> The night before she died, between eleven and twelve o'clock, she sang with a loud voice, "Hallelujah, Hallelujah, Hallelujah." About one o'clock she said to the

young person who sat up with the nurse, "The enemy
has deceived me long enough; but he shall deceive me no
more: he shall not have me. O what a deliverance! What
great grace!" Nearly two hours after, she exclaimed
aloud,—"The carriage is come! The carriage is come
for me! O what a beautiful carriage! It is come for me;
and I am coming; I am coming! O how clear the way is!
I shall soon be there. Glory! Glory! Glory! O what great
grace! Angels are come for me! Cannot you see them?
Bless the Lord! Bless the Lord!" Then turning her face
to the pillow, she said,—"O how easy! How easy!" From
that time she spoke no more to be understood; but lay
from three, till about seven o'clock, when she took her
happy flight to the joys of the Lord, on Saturday, Jan.
17, 1801.

At first it seemed improbable that a young woman could have
actually died like this—"getting happy," as it were, and embracing death as a carriage, driven by angels, come to take her
away. On the one hand it seemed outlandish. But it rang true
with me.

Working as a pastor I have been privileged with intimate
access to the interior life of faithful people engaged in the
spiritual work of dying. This experience has convinced me
that some people attain great spiritual heights as they live
out the last years of their lives and sometimes know genuine
joy—even ecstasy—as they approach the edge of death. I
remember Lorene Martin—a white woman who was married
for fifty years to a black preacher and came to my church week
after week in the last years of her life so that she could listen
to the sermon and shout "Amen!" and "Hallelujah!" from her

favorite seat in the front pew. And I remember how Frank Swenson's family decided finally to stop arguing with him over his insistence that there were angels knocking on his front door in the days before he died. I remember a friend telling me about Angela Morales, convinced as she died a painful death from cancer that she was being visited and comforted by her mother and father, each of whom had been dead for years. And I remember a colleague telling me about Cleve Wilson, whose dying words were "Praise! Praise!" Given all that I have witnessed—and remembering the countless stories told to me by others—it seems entirely plausible to me that Mrs. Hunter died the way J. Wood said she did.

Most people I know—including many who routinely work with the dying—are baffled when they meet someone who approaches the end of life with a generalized sense of well-being, and whose preparation for dying includes experiences of deep spiritual satisfaction. Unable to explain this kind of contentedness in the face of death, clinical professionals commonly misdiagnose a chronic case of "denial" and of course attribute any sightings of angels and the like to dementia. I see this same misunderstanding in family members puzzled by the happiness of their dying loved ones. Laura Osgood, at sixty, simply couldn't believe that her ninety-year-old mother, Janelle Kennedy, was as happy as she professed to be, while living "all alone in that big old house." Carol Corcoran, reeling from the anticipated loss of her husband, Mark, couldn't believe that Mark was so cheerful and contented—albeit sometimes deliriously so—as he died from cancer.

These people baffle us because they are, in their own way, practicing a ritualized way of dying that has been lost to our conscious remembrance. When we encounter it anew it can, at first, seem shocking and nonsensical. But people live and die by drawing on the spiritual resources that have been passed down to them from their mentors in life and faith. One of my parishioners, Tom Callen, put it this way after witnessing his mother Lucille's inspiring death: "I will take that moment with me to my grave." I do not doubt that he will.

The modern reader may be inclined to hear in all this some degree of wishful thinking—on the part of J. Wood and the other authors of the accounts of happy deaths, or perhaps on my own. But the ritual of the happy death was well established long before the editors of religious magazines like *The Arminian* began making accounts of these deaths a staple of their publications. Indeed, as this book will show, the ritual traces back to the testimonies of the early Christian martyrs, and indeed to the death of Jesus himself. While of course it has ebbed and flowed in popularity, and taken on varied cultural incarnations, the ritual has proven across the ages a remarkably lasting witness to the true meaning of human life and death.

Neither is the ritual's continued practice a figment of my imagination. In the course of writing this book I have had occasion to share with hundreds of people my experiences with the ritual of happy dying. Invariably, others will say to me, "that reminds me of my grandfather," or "I once had a friend who died like that." When I share Mrs. Hunter's story with my colleagues in pastoral ministry, and others who work with the dying, they all have their own experiences to share. There are a whole host of people practicing their own versions of this ancient ritual in our day.

Mrs. Hunter was clearly a product of her times. Her language, her theology, her view of the world—none of these can be artificially re-created in the twenty-first century. On the one hand, she will remain forever frozen in time.

But on the other hand, Mrs. Hunter's witness is timeless. Her happy death is a case study for the ages, a template, of sorts, for a way of approaching life and death that has been practiced for centuries and can have great meaning for present and future generations.

The people whose stories I tell in this book are witnesses to this same way of life and death. In their own vernacular, and in their own rhythms and cadences, they were, in the days that I was privileged to know them, practicing a historic ritual. They have been—to use another phrase of Mrs. Hunter's—as angels come for me. I hope that because their dying days are now accounted for, we, too, can learn the lessons they have to teach in their holy lives and happy deaths.

PART 1

MRS. HUNTER'S HAPPY DEATH

lowing his

1

WHATEVER DEGREE OF GRACE: SHARING GOD'S GREATEST GIFT

Whatever degree of Grace is communicated by the Lord Jesus Christ, the Head of the Church, to any individual, is not intended for the good of that person only, but that he might shine as a light in the family, the church and the world.

— J. WOOD

I have known a few people who died with a spirit of apparent nonchalance, but for most the approach of death raises gut-level questions about the true meaning of life. Is there a God? What kind of God? And what are we, as human beings, that God should care about us? Can we really hope to know God in this life? . . . in the next?

The world's great religious traditions answer these questions

All quoted passages by J. Wood are taken from "An Account of Mrs. Hunter's Holy Life and Happy Death."

by asserting that the fundamental nature of God is characterized by grace. The Hebrew word *hesed,* or "mercy," appears over two hundred times in the Old Testament, and the Greek equivalent, *charis*—translated as "grace"—over one hundred times in the much shorter New Testament. As a friend of mine once explained it to me, "Grace means there's nothing you can do to make God love you more, and there's nothing you can do to make God love you less. God loves you. That's the beginning and the ending of your story and mine."

The story of Mrs. Hunter's holy life and happy death is rooted firmly in this biblical tradition. J. Wood tips his hand in the very first words of his account: he is about to introduce a woman who was determined to communicate in her living and dying the grace made known to her in her twenty-six years of life.

———

Mary Hunter's death at the age of twenty-six may strike us as premature, but her fate was entirely common among people living in England and America in the seventeenth and eighteenth centuries.

Death in infancy and early childhood was a matter of course, as is made clear by the experience of Cotton Mather, the Massachusetts clergyman famous for his role in the Salem witch trials of 1692: Mather fathered fourteen children, but seven died as infants and another at age two. Or consider the case of John and Charles Wesley, the brothers who in eighteenth-century England founded the religious movement known as Methodism. John and Charles were two of nineteen children born to Samuel and Susanna Wesley, but only ten reached adolescence and John was given names—John and Benjamin—of older siblings who had died soon after birth.

Neither did surviving childhood guarantee longevity in Mrs. Hunter's day. Women were especially vulnerable during their childbearing years, and with the industrial revolution advancing rapidly, living and working conditions in England's cities were notorious. Disease ran rampant and popular folk remedies were widely practiced, often with devastating consequences: bleeding was still a common treatment for routine infections; drinking lye was believed to help cleanse the body of ulcers and tumors; smoking tobacco was common for easing the pains of toothaches and the like. Hospitals offered little help—not yet institutionalized as establishments for the study and cure of illness, they were run, in the historian Jacques Barzun's estimation, as "indiscriminate refuges for the poor and the sick."

Mary Hunter lived more than one hundred years after Thomas Hobbes had issued his famous indictment of life in the modern era: "No arts, no letters, no society, and which is worst of all, continual fear and danger of violent death, and the life of man solitary, poor, nasty, brutish, and short." Hobbes's words would remain famous for generations, however, because they seemed so entirely apt.

Against this backdrop it made sense that even vibrant young men and women would choose to cast their lives in the light of the prospect of death.

Something curious was happening, though, in the world of English-speaking Christianity in the generations that spanned the seventeenth and eighteenth centuries. People were not living longer—death was as present and potent as ever—but the *fear* of death seemed to be subsiding in the popular imagination. The change was perceptible in English graveyards, where—as the historian David Stannard has shown—more and more tombstones featured engravings of sunrises or angels' wings, instead of the traditional skull-shaped "death's head." It was noticeable in the preaching of the eighteenth century's great revivalists, too, who were gradually shifting their emphasis from the traditional threats of eternal damnation to such sayings as John Wesley's "All people can be saved; all people can know they are saved; all people can be saved to the uttermost." It could be heard in church music too, where the optimistic hymns of John's genius brother Charles were beginning to dominate.

The uplifting doctrine to which the Wesleys were giving popular expression went by the name "Free Grace," the title of one of Charles's favorite hymns. This doctrine asserted that an individual's salvation could be had by God's grace alone and could not be achieved by any human endeavor. This sentiment had fueled the Protestant Reformation on the European continent—so called for its adherents' "protests" against the perceived abuses of the Roman Catholic Church. In England the same impulse had given rise to an era of Puritan reform, whose adherents wanted to "purify" the beliefs and practices of the Church of England. Protestants and Puritans alike understood that the gift of grace was entirely unmerited: as the contemporary preacher George Regas has said of God's grace, "you can't earn it, you can't buy it, you can't win it, you can't deserve it—all you can do is accept it."

So it was that by the time Mary Hunter died a happy death

in 1801, she had behind her generations of religious ferment. She had been taught that God's grace alone was sufficient for her salvation, and she had available for her inspiration a treasure trove of hymns, stories, and sermons, and the examples set by countless others who had died before her in the faith. Having had the grace of God communicated to her so powerfully, she came to view her dying as presenting a golden opportunity to convey this same grace to others.

———————

A few years into my tenure as the pastor of Westchester United Methodist Church, a midsized congregation on the west side of Los Angeles, a couple named Jim and Barbara Wislocki started coming to church. In his fifties, of English and Polish ancestry, with a round face but a pointed nose, Jim was as outgoing as his wife was shy. More than once after Sunday worship, over a cup of coffee and between pleasantries exchanged with other members of the congregation, Jim and I debriefed the day's sermon while Barbara politely listened in.

Jim was a theological novice, but he had an active and inquisitive mind. An engineer with a strong background in science, he was pleased to find that I was willing to entertain rationalist critiques of the Bible and was interested to explore how I, as a Christian pastor, might account for the spiritual renewal he was experiencing at this time in his life.

As he explained it to me, it had all begun with his meeting Barbara, who had loved him in a way that he had not believed he was capable of being loved. "I've done some awful things in my life," he told me on more than one occasion, "but Barbara just refused to let the past get in the way."

Through Barbara, Jim was experiencing what Charles Wesley, almost three centuries earlier, had called "free grace." For Jim, estranged from his first wife and their two grown children, meeting and marrying Barbara had marked the beginning of a whole new life.

At first Jim had believed he was going to church for Barbara's sake, but week by week he found that what he was hearing and experiencing on Sunday mornings was resonating with his own spirit. He asked to become a member of the church and began to call himself a Christian, something he confessed he would have considered, at an earlier stage of life, to be a laughable impossibility.

About a year after joining the church, Jim was diagnosed with cancer—a CAT scan had revealed a malignant tumor growing beneath his skull, behind his left ear. A few weeks later he called me up and asked if I could tell him why he wasn't depressed. I couldn't, of course, but when he told me he was preparing to undergo intensive chemotherapy, I assumed he was mustering a kind of optimism that I had seen before in cancer patients. In my experience, this kind of optimism serves people well, so I offered Jim nothing but encouragement. "I don't know why you're feeling so upbeat," I said, "but I say just run with it."

Something about Jim, though, was different from most cancer patients I had known. Through the course of his treatment, his spiritual awakening accelerated. In the midst of a taxing regimen of chemotherapy and radiation, he was absolutely blooming. He was in love with his wife—"the best wife anyone could ever want." He was in love with his new church—"a great church, a fantastic group of people." He was in love with life.

Knowing that Jim was something of a computer expert, I called him up one day, explained to him that I was in the market for a new laptop, and asked his advice.

"Let's go shopping," he proposed. I was quick to accept the invitation.

The next Wednesday I drove up to the front of Jim's house and, per our agreement, honked the horn. As he walked to the car, I noticed he had lost a lot of weight, something that, ironically, made his entirely average middle-aged paunch stand out more than it ever had before. He smiled at me and tipped his plaid racing cap—his preferred sartorial strategy for hiding the patchy baldness that chemotherapy had caused.

Jim and I drove to Westwood, to a little computer store that dealt in high volume with faculty and students at nearby UCLA. Jim was on a mission to get me the best laptop money could buy.

After I insisted again and again that I really did need to work within a budget, Jim finally relented. He asked a salesman to start up a couple of different models and took them for a test drive while I looked over his shoulder.

After talking me through a comparison, Jim pointed at the second laptop on the counter and said, "This is a great computer. This is the best value. This will last you a long, long time." Six years later, when I first sat down to type out Jim's story on my Toshiba Satellite 315CDS, I remarked that he was entirely right.

After shopping we drove down the coast and stopped for lunch at a fish house in Marina del Rey. Sitting on the restaurant's sunlit veranda, eating a swordfish sandwich, Jim could hardly contain himself. This was an absolutely incredible day. I had just bought what was arguably the best laptop computer in the world (under $1,500, anyway). We were eating the best swordfish ever caught. Our view of the Pacific was unsurpassed. Surely I had to agree with him: life just doesn't get any better than this.

Jim Wislocki, dying of cancer, was treating me to one of the best days of his life. It was one of the best days of my life too.

That week I determined to pay closer attention to Jim. For several months my own spirit at church had been growing worse and worse. I was bickering with some of the church's leaders—over what I can now barely recall—and I had let these disagreements sour my mood. I decided to try to look at the church through Jim's eyes, to see if I could account for his unabashed enthusiasm.

At the coffee hour the following Sunday, Jim worked the room as if he were the pastor, not I. He welcomed newcomers, singing the praises of his new church family and bragging about my preaching. He consoled the people, sick or grieving, whose names had been lifted during the time of public prayer.

Even the people I experienced as most difficult Jim found delightful. He called me over to hear a story that Dave Lovell was telling him, not knowing that Dave and I had been engaged in a bitter argument just the week before. With Jim egging him on, Dave started the story over and when he finished, the three of us laughed and laughed.

Over the course of the next few weeks I stayed in close touch with Jim Wislocki. It dawned on me that I was sick in spirit, and Jim's infectious grace was the perfect remedy. Following his lead, I began once again to practice the simple discipline of looking for the best in people, instead of expecting the worst. My heart softened.

Eventually, Jim gave up on chemotherapy. The tumor had not responded to treatment and was continuing to spread. His oncologist said surgery was not an option because the tumor was deeply enmeshed with his brain. He would continue with radiation, to delay the cancer's spread, but he stopped all curative measures in hopes of improving the quality of his remaining weeks or months.

At this point in his life Jim astonished me. Quite simply, he displayed no fear or apprehension in the face of death. In fact, apart from the thought of leaving Barbara, he did not give any real signs of lament. Every day was better than before, filled with remarkable surprises and unexpected gifts. As his body died from cancer, Jim's spirit was being filled to the brim with life and love.

In his last weeks, Jim was overcome by a sense of oneness with God. I asked him what he thought about dying, and, a scientist through and through, he said he conceived of it like this: "It is all energy and mass. And if I live or if I die, I will still be a part of the cosmos, I will still be a part of God. I will have changed in form but I will not cease to be." Jim's formulation struck me as an authentic attempt to put into modern language the inexpressible, inescapable mystery of God's immeasurable grace. As Christians the world over sing almost weekly in worship, "Glory be to the Father, and to the Son, and to the Holy Ghost. As it was in the beginning, is now and ever shall be, world without end, Amen."

A few weeks after his death, I remembered Jim in a Mother's Day sermon at church. I shared with people how Barbara, by "refusing to let the past get in the way," had demonstrated for Jim the very essence of God's grace. And I shared how blessed I had been by Jim's readiness to share that same grace with me.

I wish I had known then, though, what I know now. Were I to preach that sermon today I would be able to trace in great detail the lineage of Jim Wislocki's spirit. It is exactly the same spirit evidenced by Mary Hunter and her peers as they died their happy deaths near the turn of the nineteenth century.

Of course Mrs. Hunter would not have understood the first thing about Jim's talk of energy and mass. They were born two centuries apart, and their views of the natural order of things—the "way the world works"—could not have been more different.

But Mrs. Hunter would have understood perfectly Jim's ever-increasing awareness of God's grace as the foundation of his life. And she would have understood just what Jim was doing as he lavished affection on his newfound friends at church: he was sharing grace with others because grace was the very best gift he himself had ever received.

And Mrs. Hunter would have understood perfectly the sense of spiritual fulfillment Jim Wislocki knew as he approached the edge of death. She described it this way in her journal:

> My soul longs for a fuller union with God ... O for
> more of this uninterrupted tranquility of soul! I have, as
> yet, but a drop from the ocean of eternal happiness.

The week before I first preached that sermon I called Barbara, to ask how she was doing and to tell her I was planning to talk about Jim in church. At the end of our conversation I asked if we could sing a hymn or two in Jim's honor during worship that Sunday. Barbara made two selections, including Charles Wesley's most famous and triumphant hymn:

> *O for a thousand tongues to sing my great Redeemer's praise.*
> *The glories of his majesty, the triumphs of his grace!*

Had I told the people in church that day that the hymn was of Barbara's choosing, I'm sure they would have been puzzled. Why would she pick this song—so upbeat, so happy—after having just lost to death the love of her life?

But I was privileged to know Jim Wislocki in his living and in his dying. And I know Barbara got things exactly right.

2

TO SHINE IN A SUFFERING STATE:
THIS LITTLE LIGHT OF MINE

Hence it becomes a duty in the receiver to communicate to his Christian friends, while he is able to attend to the worship of God; and when deprived of this privilege, to shine in a suffering state.

— J. WOOD

Because he was, for the most part, secretive about his past, I never learned much about Jim Wislocki's upbringing. I cannot say if he was raised in any particular religious tradition, nor whether he was reclaiming any specific part of his family's heritage as he died a happy death. What I can say for certain is this: Jim Wislocki was not the first person to experience a sense of spiritual transcendence as he approached the edge of death—far from it. In fact, the ritual of happy dying has deep, deep roots, the chain of its cultural transmission dating back to the earliest generations of the Christian movement.

In Mrs. Hunter's England the happy death was most strongly

associated with the Methodists, renegade members of the Church of England. The Methodists claimed to have inherited the tradition from their Puritan forebears, who considered the willingness to die for a cause a sign of true faith. In fact, many Puritans had been martyred in the sixteenth and seventeenth centuries for their opposition to the English crown, and their stories were the stuff of legend in Mrs. Hunter's day. Typical is the story of William Tyndale, famous for translating the Bible into English, and burned at the stake in 1536 for this treason. Tyndale's dying words were a prayer for his enemy: "Lord—open the King of England's eyes."

But the legacy of happy dying went far beyond the British Isles and the era of Puritan reform. A tradition known as *Ars Moriendi* (the Art of Dying), which had flourished throughout Europe in the fourteenth and fifteenth centuries, consisted of the stories of characters who, while commonly afflicted by deathbed torments and fears, always succeeded in finding peace, encouragement, and consolation at the threshold of death. And for centuries faithful Catholics had been concluding their daily prayers with the "Night Prayer" or Compline, signing off with this request: "May the Lord almighty grant us a quiet night and a happy death."

Many of the saints from the Middle Ages were also said to have died happy deaths. To cite just one example, the renowned church historian known as the Venerable Bede died in the year 735, while completing a dictated translation of the gospel of John. A companion wrote up a celebrated account of the monk's happy death: after he supplied the last sentence of the gospel, Bede declared his work finished, then sat upon the floor of his monastery cell singing, "Glory be to the Father and to the Son and to the Holy Ghost" until, peacefully, he breathed his last breath.

Going back even further, the history of the earliest Christians was filled with the stories of monks and martyrs who experienced a sense of spiritual communion with God as they approached the edge of death. The martyrs were heralded for displaying a spirit of transcendence, even while being executed, and for encouraging and consoling the onlooking crowd. They found scriptural warrant for this posture of spiritual confidence in the first letter of Peter: "and if ye suffer for righteousness' sake, happy are ye; and be not afraid of their terror, and neither be troubled; But sanctify the Lord God in your hearts: and be ready always to give an answer to every man that asketh you a reason of the hope that is in you" (I Peter 3:14–15).

The staying power of the ritual of the happy death is no coincidence: across cultures and generations, its practitioners have believed themselves to be replicating in their own lives the pattern of Christ himself, who underwent the extreme physical rigors of crucifixion with a spirit of confident assurance. His famous last words could be read by some as expressions of lament—"Not my will, but thy will be done"; "Father, forgive them, for they know not what they do"—but to the ears of those who practiced the happy death they also conveyed a supreme confidence in God. Christ's final utterance—"It is finished"—was similarly open to interpretation. On the one hand it can be heard as referring to the extinguishment of life, but on the other it can be heard as referring to the completion of a race by one ready now to receive a prize.

Even Christ's darkest utterance—"My God, my God, why hast thou forsaken me?"—portrayed so dramatically in Catho-

lic renderings of the "last words of Christ," sounded different
to those who practiced the ritual of the happy death in Mrs.
Hunter's day. Christ's words were familiar to them, steeped as
they were in the poetry of the Bible and accustomed to daily
recitation of the Psalms. Surely Christ was not despairing,
they thought, but merely uttering the Twenty-second Psalm,
which turns dramatically after its familiar opening verse into a
confident song of praise:

> My God, my God, why hast thou forsaken me? why art
> thou so far from helping me, and from the words of
> my roaring? O my God, I cry in the daytime, but thou
> hearest not; and in the night season, and am not silent.
> But thou art holy, O thou that inhabitest the praises of
> Israel. Our fathers trusted in thee: they trusted, and thou
> didst deliver them. They cried unto thee, and were deliv-
> ered: they trusted in thee, and were not confounded.

So it was that many Christians living in England and
America in the seventeenth and eighteenth centuries understood themselves to be joining a great and venerable tradition.
By practicing a happy death they were, in their own small way,
following in the footsteps of the early martyrs and witnessing
to their faith (the English word "witness" is just a translation
of the Greek word *martyrios*). If they suffered great physical
pain as they died, or were ridiculed as naive by others, what
were these compared to the suffering and ridicule experienced
by earlier Christians and indeed by Christ himself?

Men and women like Mary Hunter believed that by "shining
in a suffering state" they could realize—and communicate—a
true awareness of God's grandeur and love. They practiced the

happy death in pursuit of spiritual enlightenment, for themselves and others, and they died in hopes that those dear to them, inspired by their example, would keep the faith.

———

A few months after coming across J. Wood's account of Mrs. Hunter's happy death, I witnessed the death of a remarkable woman, Lucille Callen. Eighty-four years old, but vibrant and sharp to an extraordinary degree, Lucille had moved to Anaheim, California, in the 1950s. She was one of a legion of Midwesterners to take advantage after World War II of the plentiful sunshine and opportunity on offer in "the Golden State." Lucille was a legend in the community of Anaheim, where she had occupied, across years of volunteering, virtually every leadership position in the church, the public schools, and a variety of women's organizations.

For over forty years Lucille had lived in the same house in a part of Anaheim that was once covered with orange groves. For most of that time she had shared her house with her husband, Harry, and together they raised two sons there, Tom and John. Harry had died in 1990, long before I arrived as the pastor at Anaheim United Methodist Church. About the same time, Tom had moved back in after living in Los Angeles, where he had been working as an engineer.

The reasons for Tom's move back home were entirely practical—he had muscular dystrophy, which was progressing to the point where he needed ever more assistance with the routines of daily living. In this case, magic was born of convenience: Lucille and Tom were perfectly suited to living under the same roof. As Tom grew increasingly frail, Lucille was able to care for him in the way she had cared for Harry in his old age. As Lucille's eyesight began to fail, Tom became the eyes of the family, reading his mother the newspaper and the baseball box scores each morning and tending to the family finances and correspondence. They shared passions galore: for God; for the Anaheim Angels; for friends and family; for their church; for the Democratic Party. During my four years as pastor in Anaheim, surrounded by conservative Orange County Republicans, I took political refuge in Tom and Lucille, exchanging with them e-mails, newspaper articles, and knowing glances whenever conversations at church turned to politics.

One Wednesday afternoon in the spring of 2004, Lucille began to feel a pain in her side. Two days later she went to the hospital for exploratory surgery; what the surgeons found was an intestinal cancer so widespread there was nothing that could be done.

That night, as Lucille lay dying in the hospital, I had the privilege to visit with her as she was coming out of surgery, accompanied by her sons.

Tom and John were clearly in shock. The surgeon and oncologist had met with them jointly to explain to them the results of the surgery. The cancer had completely corrupted Lucille's colon and lower intestine, to the extent that they could not be surgically repaired. Within a few hours, a day at most, Lucille would bleed to death.

I asked Lucille's sons if anyone had explained to her the results of the surgery.

"No," they said, "she is really just coming to."

"Do you want me to tell her?"

"Yes, please," they answered.

I stepped to the bedside, took hold of her hand, and called her name.

Lucille was visibly pleased to see me. Hooked up to a respirator, she was unable to speak, but she followed my words closely, nodding or shaking her head decisively in response to my inquiries.

Did she know what happened in the surgery? No. Did she want me to tell her? Yes.

I explained to Lucille what her sons had explained to me, and then said, "It won't be long, Lucille. Do you know that?" She nodded yes, and I continued with my line of questioning.

Was she in a great deal of pain? Yes. Was she afraid? No. Did she trust that God is good? Yes. Did she want to hear something from the Bible? Would she like it if I sang a hymn? Yes. Yes.

I read a few passages from the Bible and then sang a few hymns traditional to the season—it was the season of Lent, when the church is focused on the cross, and so I found myself singing songs about the death and suffering of Jesus.

I could tell that something about these hymns did not quite sit right with Lucille. I could tell that she was concerned for her sons, sitting by her bedside, and that she wanted me to sing something that would lift their spirits. I asked her a question that her sons must have thought a little odd. "Would you like me to sing something more upbeat?" Lucille nodded.

"How about a few verses from 'Morning Has Broken'?" Lucille smiled and nodded with great enthusiasm—a decisive "yes."

"Morning Has Broken" is a favorite hymn for many, many people of Lucille's generation. Made popular outside church circles in the 1960s by the folk singer Cat Stevens, the lyrics were written in 1931 by Eleanor Farjeon and put to a traditional Gaelic melody. I sang:

> Morning has broken, like the first morning;
> Blackbird has spoken, like the first bird;
> Praise for the singing, praise for the morning,
> Praise for them, springing fresh from the Word.

Lucille brightened visibly at the singing of this hymn and nodded her affirmation and appreciation. In fact, she nodded her head up and down perceptibly to the beat. I continued to sing:

> Mine is the sunlight! Mine is the morning
> Born of the one light Eden saw play!
> Praise with elation, praise every morning,
> God's re-creation of the new day!

As I finished Lucille turned her head, a smile on her face and her eyes filled with tears, and set her gaze upon her sons. She died a few hours later, just before midnight.

One week later, at Lucille's funeral, her son John would recall this moment in his eulogy:

> I am not an evangelical Christian . . . But I am a Witness:
> I have seen the Lord. I have seen the Lord, leaning over
> my mother's hospital bed, bending close so she could
> hear and see him. I watched her gaze up at Him, her
> expression changing from pain to love. She saw Him,
> too.

> It was her pastor who had walked into the ICU and greeted us who were gathered around her bed, but it was God that spoke to her, welcoming her, spoke to us, comforting us. Mercy filled the room that night. God's hand reached through our paralyzing grief and led Mom quickly through the valley of the shadow of death.

What John and Tom witnessed that night was not just a pastor praying deathbed prayers and singing familiar hymns. They also witnessed what was so commonly reported in the accounts of happy deaths from the turn of the nineteenth century: God filling a room with mercy and a faithful person shining forth in the moment of her death.

Though I did not sing it with her that night in the hospital, another song I know Lucille knew by heart is the one we sang every Sunday at the Anaheim church as the children came forward to the front of the sanctuary for a time with the pastor:

> *This little light of mine, I'm going to let it shine,*
> *Let it shine, let it shine, let it shine.*

For most people of faith, that we should "let our light shine" seems little more than common sense. But it does not occur to most in our day that the dying, too, are capable, as J. Wood put it, of "shining in a suffering state." For the practitioners of the happy death, though, from Mrs. Hunter to Lucille Callen, to shine this way in the moment of dying is nothing less than a duty—a duty requiring great pain and struggle, but a joyful duty nonetheless, a duty born of love.

3

HANDED DOWN TO POSTERITY: THE LIFE OF A STORY

The light of truth and holiness appearing in the last stage of life should be carefully collected for the good of surviving relatives, and, when proper, handed down to posterity.

— J. WOOD

While the obituary pages remain among the most popular pages in newspapers like the *New York Times,* few of us today would consider appropriate the publication of a detailed account of a loved one's dying days. Still, a great many people take the time to write accounts like this—I hear them presented regularly as a part of the eulogies shared at church funerals and graveside services. J. Wood's account of Mrs. Hunter's happy death is certainly longer and more verbose than the typical modern eulogy, but its function is identical: to share good words about God by sharing good words about the recently deceased.

In preparing for funerals I commonly ask the family and friends of the deceased to help me prepare by writing down their thoughts and memories. Most often people respond to this request with great enthusiasm. Typically someone in the family will say, "I've already started to write something down." Often more than one person will choose to write a eulogy, even if not all choose to share at the funeral what they've written at home. And often these written eulogies will include detailed stories of the loved one's final days.

Of course the act of writing serves a therapeutic effect for the author, as a thousand books on journaling can attest. But this kind of writing is also routinely experienced by others as a gift. I know from both personal and professional experience that eulogies spoken at funerals are commonly circulated in written form for years, even decades, among family members and friends. These eulogies—like the accounts of Mrs. Hunter's day—are often "handed down to posterity," their wisdom passed down from one generation to the next. The story of a life can be a beautiful thing to share. And the life of a story can be lasting and profound.

People living in Mrs. Hunter's day were expert at sharing the stories of their loved ones' deaths, writing them up and sharing them at funerals and in personal journals, diaries, and letters. But tales from the deathbed were considered more than the stuff of personal correspondence—courage in the face of death, an age-old theme, remained a staple in the literature of the day. Biographical portraits of the Puritan heroes had been for generations among the most popular books in England—from John Foxe's *Acts and Monuments* to Thomas Fuller's *The History of the Worthies of England* and Samuel Clarke's *The Lives of Sundry Eminent Persons in this Later Age*. And on both sides of the Atlantic, proponents of happy dying filled periodicals of every imaginable kind with glowing obituaries and uplifting accounts from the deathbed. Had Jim Wislocki and Lucille Callen lived and died at the turn of the nineteenth century, their stories would have been considered prime material for publication.

The religious press of the eighteenth and nineteenth centuries was an extraordinarily influential institution, and with advances in printing technologies, the number of publications proliferated on both sides of the Atlantic. From its inception as a bimonthly magazine in 1778, *The Arminian* was among the most popular magazines in England. In America *The Arminian's* weekly counterpart, *The Christian Advocate*, shattered circulation records, its readership growing from 28,000 in 1828 to 120,000 in 1841. "The Advocate," as its readers called it, remained among the most popular weekly publications in America for most of its 150-year history.

Written up by the pastors, spouses, and friends of the deceased, the stories of "happy deaths" were presented in different formats in different publications. In local newspapers they were folded into brief obituaries. In magazines like *The Arminian* or *The Advocate*, they were sometimes published as part of longer biographies—entitled "experiences" or "memoirs" or simply "The Life of Mr. So-and-So." When they were published as freestanding items, they were labeled "accounts."

Accounts of happy deaths were featured articles in any number of religious publications through the middle of the nineteenth century. For the first half century of the *Arminian's* publication, accounts like J. Wood's were the lead articles in the magazine and sometimes constituted a near majority of the magazine's pages. It is hard to overemphasize this fact, or the truth it illustrates: some months all other topics combined warranted barely as much attention, in the view of the *Arminian*'s editors, as did these accounts of ordinary people dying exemplary deaths.

J. Wood's "An Account of Mrs. Hunter's Holy Life and Happy Death" is representative of the genre in almost every way. Published in two installments—in the magazine's July and August issues in 1801—the eleven-page account provides biographic detail only insofar as it assists in driving the account to the inevitable conclusion of Mrs. Hunter's happy death. J. Wood offers no physical description of his subject and says nothing of interests, hobbies, or affections except those evidencing her religious faith. The account provides very little insight into what today we would call Mrs. Hunter's "personal life." Apart from an opening mention of "the late Mr. Clulow," we read nothing about Mrs. Hunter's father. The account includes just two passing references to her husband, and while it makes reference to "her little ones and other domestic duties," Mrs. Hunter's children are never numbered or named.

Even Mrs. Hunter herself is oddly anonymous: there is but a single mention of her first name, Mary—recorded in the blessing she received at her mother's deathbed, as will be discussed in Chapter 7 of this book. Throughout the account J. Wood calls his star witness to the possibilities of happy dying, quite simply, "Mrs. Hunter." In effect he cultivates an air of secrecy about his subject, even as he idealizes and idolizes her.

On the one hand, J. Wood's determination to conceal a number of things about his subject's identity (and, indeed, his own) reflects the formality of the day. On the other hand, it points to a larger understanding: as an author he is not heralding and celebrating Mrs. Hunter because she was so unique a woman. He considers the story of her life and death worthy of publication and emulation precisely because she was, in most ways, an "everywoman." She was, as J. Wood chose to portray her, an ordinary woman who lived a remarkably faithful life and died an extraordinarily faithful death.

———————

J. Wood professes to be little more than an editor of Mrs. Hunter's own journal, writing:

> I shall endeavour to give as faithful an account of Mrs. Hunter, as possible; and I shall have the less difficulty in this as she left in her own hand writing some information respecting her conversion, her sorrows, and consolations. I shall, therefore, have little more to do than transcribe from her own papers, except here and there to add a few words by way of elucidation.

The protestation notwithstanding, his editorial control is decisive in giving the account its focus and shape. He carefully chooses excerpts from Mrs. Hunter's journal to tell the story of her journey in the Christian faith, and when her journal falls silent, he imagines that "there is good reason to hope that this was not from any loss she had suffered in her Christian experience." Elsewhere he summarizes whole swaths of her journey by reassuring his readers that "her growth in grace was considerable [and] that she was visibly ripening for the heavenly garner." Later in the account he will try to justify his editorial decision making, saying:

> Much larger extracts might have been made from Mrs.
> Hunter's memorandums: but on account of the same-
> ness of ideas and expressions ... I have laboured to be
> sparing herein, especially as she had not the most happy
> way of expressing her thoughts with her pen.

This condescension seems laughable in light of his own senti-mental and hyperbolic prose.

J. Wood's account is similar, in the finest detail, to thou-sands of accounts of happy deaths published in the late eigh-teenth and early nineteenth centuries. In the months following my discovery of it, I read hundreds of others like it. J. Wood's manner of concluding his tale, in particular, conforms to a formula that was almost universal to the accounts—he records her dying utterances, describes her final moments, and affirms the happiness of her spirit, before closing with a biographical or literary flourish.

Even those unable to profess their happiness had it attrib-uted to them, as it was in "An Account of the Experience and Death of Mrs. Hannah Wood, of Manchester":

> The next day her speech was taken from her by a
> stroke of the palsy, so that she could not speak to be
> understood:—Nevertheless, by signs to her friends, she
> intimated, that the consolations of Christ abounded,
> and that she was continually happy in his Love. The day
> before her death, she partook of the Lord's Supper, and
> was abundantly refreshed in spirit;—her countenance

was changed [such] that it seemed as if glory shone in
her face. She continued in this frame till Sept. 30, when
she resigned her happy spirit into the hands of God.

Modern readers may be inclined to hear in all this more
than a little bit of exaggeration. Isn't it possible that this whole
ritual of happy dying was really an exercise in wishful thinking on the part of those grieving the loss of their loved ones?
Isn't it possible that J. Wood and the other authors of these
accounts were simply projecting their own desires onto their
dying subjects?

Had I not found in these accounts the echoes of things I had
witnessed in my work as a pastor, I might have been inclined to
dismiss them—as have many professional historians—as the
fanciful literary creations of people steeped in a death-denying
culture. But narratives like J. Wood's account of Mrs. Hunter's
happy death reminded me powerfully of events I had witnessed
in my own life and ministry, and so I found it unsatisfactory to
simply refuse them their say. Slowly but surely, I became accustomed to the authors' usage of the English language. I learned,
in time, to read *through* the accounts, as if looking through a
slightly opaque window, to catch illuminating glimpses of life
and death in the year 1801. I learned not to take the accounts
at face value, but rather to take them on their own terms. I
came to understand that, while of course the accounts both reported and reflected the spirit of their age, they also captured
powerfully a spirit of "happiness" that transcended their time.
As I immersed myself in them I found between their lines the
spirit of people I had known and loved.

Writing like J. Wood's cannot be classified using contemporary categories. The process of recalling and recording events

fraught with emotion and spiritual significance is far more fluid and complex than the contemporary categories of "fiction" and "nonfiction" allow. This kind of writing takes on vastly different shape in differing cultural contexts. J. Wood saw Mrs. Hunter's story as evidence of the possibilities for Christian living and dying. By sharing his rendition of it he was contributing to a well-established body of literature, a body of literature that was explicitly evangelistic and promoted a very particular, religious worldview. But he was not simply inventing things, and he was not merely "spinning a yarn." He was "accounting" for Mrs. Hunter's death, attempting to cope with the reality of her death and explain what made it possible for her to die with such remarkable grace. He was confident that his tale would encourage others to follow Mrs. Hunter's example—"if she can do it," he seems to be saying, "you can too."

J. Wood was not simply "making things up" as he shared his account. Neither were Mrs. Hunter and her contemporaries "just pretending" to be happy as they labored toward death. As perceptive historians have shown, both the dying and the accounting of it were parts of a coherent religious ritual. That accounts of people's happy deaths were published so proudly served to reinforce the practice of the ritual itself. I do not doubt for a second that Mrs. Hunter suspected the story of her dying stood a good chance of being published in her favorite religious magazine. She was putting into practice exactly what she had been taught: to live and die—in the words of one Charles Gloyne, describing the death of his wife in the March 1801 issue of *The Arminian*—"as one who must give an account."

One of the most moving eulogies I have ever read was never spoken aloud, and in fact was never circulated beyond the author's immediate family until I asked for permission to include it in this book. Entitled "God's Token of Love," it was written in 1968 by Dawn Moore, who was then the secretary at Anaheim Methodist Church. It tells the story of the death of Donny Moore, Dawn's twelve-year-old son:

> Donny's Pot of Gold came a little before he got to the end of his rainbow. From the reflection of the sunshine in his smile you would never have known the contents were green instead of gold.
>
> When Donny was just two months past his eleventh birthday, he began feeling ill. I would find him lying down, dizzy and nauseated. A check-up found nothing special but it happened again and again—and interfered greatly with him being the boy he was. Ball games and roughhousing with the boys didn't take first place anymore. Lying down did.
>
> Donny loved three things—living, being a boy, and just any kind of a ball. To him one meant the other two. Legs were to run. An arm was to throw. Hands were to hold a bat. A body was to tackle. A face was to get red from sun or hard play or else dirty from being close to Mother Earth. Our tree in the parkway habitually braced itself for a body with long legs wrapping around the branches and the dichondra lawn finally gave up to the steady base sliding of sneakers and blue jeans.

Double vision crept in and I took Donny for an eye exam. When the doctor had my young son sit in the waiting room while he talked to me, I felt a vague fear. But I was unprepared for the shock that came when he kindly explained that there was a pressure that might mean a tumor. A quick appointment with a neurosurgeon and tests at a hospital proved the suspicion.

The following days of more tests and preparation for surgery seemed endless but in reality all too few, for when the surgeon came down from the operating room he said the tumor was a wild kind that could grow back.

The surgery itself was a success. But it and the involvement of the tumor and brain did leave after-effects that made Donny think for a while he had turned into something stupid. His words just wouldn't come out right. He'd talk his ever-loving baseball talk and giggle because he couldn't pronounce Minnesota (as in Minnesota Twins). He would start—grin, skip Minnesota in favor of just "Twins." He kept his sense of humor and was a good sport about his awkwardness.

By May 1967 he was back in school. Bald-headed—one eye covered with a black eye patch (to help the weakened eye) and a right leg that put his foot down in a different spot than where he had aimed. His teacher and class were great. I'd leave him for the two allowed hours and go back to find a couple of boys—they all took turns—arms supporting their pal—laughing and cutting up all the way down the walk to the car. Donny's grades had been so good that he was allowed to come to class for these few hours, share verbally and qualify for graduation from the 6th grade.

He exercised his hand continually, squeezing a hard ball—his hair grew in from being shaved for surgery and then came out again from the cobalt treatments. Long hair wasn't in style yet, but his bald head and black eye patch drew attention. If a remark was made Donny never showed that it hurt him. He flashed the same charismatic smile he'd been using for over 11 years.

During the summer a blessed man who was a friend of our family promised him a fishing trip when he could prove he could haul in the fish himself and keep his balance in the boat. Donny was ready almost immediately and invited a buddy along. They out-fished their senior friend and came home happy, sunburned, and smelly, plus fish.

Summer flew and each day his will and determination to get back in the ball game made me forget there could be anything else in his future.

By Fall he registered for Junior High. My job hours permitted me to pick him up after school. It was a six block walk to home and he deserved a ride after a day of changing classes, getting bumped in the halls, and straining to write fast enough. At first teachers seemed unaware that he had to actually draw each letter and homework was a frustrating task. But he had as much patience as the teacher and kept up. Then came January. Again the headaches, neck tightness, eye problems and nausea. The same dreadful terrifying symptoms of one year ago.

Back to the hospital and an operation to relieve whatever was causing pressure. It turned out to be just a clot
under the skull, not even involved with the brain. But
Donny failed to get better. He had new problems and
couldn't keep anything down. As days went by I asked
for permission to take him home.

I hoped he would feel better there. Maybe he was
just tired and frightened of hospitals. At home, though,
he began to lose the use of one arm. Now the doctor
told me that the tumor had returned—this time to
the spinal column and there was nothing that could be
done. In desperation I took him to another hospital that
specializes in catastrophic diseases. They used a new
chemical but made no promises. A few weeks of very
tender loving care there went by, but no improvement.
So I took him home, where he begged to be. This time
to keep him as comfortable as possible and to share, as
a family, his sickness as we so beneficially had shared in
his health.

In the short weeks that followed all use of his limbs
disappeared, and he was even unable to move his head.
We borrowed a hospital bed and rented or were given
extra equipment he needed. Two loving neighbor nurses
came to help daily. Another even followed him from
the last hospital on her own. My mother gave him in-
jections for pain as only a grandmother can. Donny's
fishing friend dropped by sometimes twice a day to do
whatever he could to comfort him. Friends, teachers,
buddies visited, read to him, sent cards and arranged
for two California Angel baseball players to come. A
star football player from high school, who had visited

after the first trip home from the hospital, came again to encourage him. Donny had not given up his desire to get well and play ball again. His favorite request was for baseball cards, and the bubble-gum that came along soon stacked up.

Then one day a sweet elderly couple came from our church. They brought his Pot of Gold in the form of a new wallet with 20 new bright green one-dollar bills inside. I will never forget the picture of the wife walking back to the car. She stopped to actually stomp and kick the ground a little, she was so upset to see Donny this way. She is such a sweet little lady and the sight of her displaying this emotion touched me deeply. In the house Donny was crying softly—he was so happy with the generous gift and the dearness of the couple. Right then he bade us get a catalogue and asked anyone who came near to turn the pages slowly so he could examine every item on each page, all the while looking for just the right thing to buy with his treasure. He would make a decision and then discard it. We would start at the front and go through again. It was quite a task holding that big catalogue up for him at just the right angle and turning each page, giving him plenty of time to look. Now every day was a brand new day for him to plan. He had been given more than twenty one-dollar bills. He had been given ideas, interests and tomorrows. The rest of us had just been keeping him comfortable and referring vaguely to the future. He was now experiencing the ability and desire to dream of something good. It renewed his desire to be—and how it kept his still active mind working and stretching!

Finally Donny chose to spend some of the money on a Monopoly Game. Then the same day he decided against it. He could not move any of the pieces nor could he set up the board so he could see to tell us how to move for him. So we started all over again with turning the pages. The end of the rainbow was getting nearer now, for he suddenly insisted that I deposit the money in the bank. There was a great hurry for me to make the transaction and return. He seemed most anxious for me to show him the bank book so he could see it was all safe. A few days later Donny reached the end of his rainbow. I'm sure God met him to guide him through the more brilliant reds, yellows, greens, blues, indigos and violets in a very real fulfillment of God's token of love.

Donald Ray Moore

11–7–55   5–25–68

As improbable as it may seem, Dawn Moore, in the midst of great emotional anguish, saw in her dying son a happiness of spirit, evidenced in the sunshine in his smile, his good humor in the face of physical illness, and his delight in small pleasures like fishing trips, baseball cards, and crisp green dollar bills— what Dawn called "God's tokens of love." And so she set out to "account for" Donny's death by writing up the tale of his dying, so mixed with bitterness and sweetness, with darkness and light. In the midst of her writing she found within the utterly tragic death of her son the light of great holiness. As counterintuitive as it may seem, her son's death brought to Dawn's mind the most beautiful of God's creations, the rainbow, an almost universal sign of hope and fulfillment.

People living in Mrs. Hunter's time would not have been

surprised by all of this. They believed that a fullness or "happiness" of spirit was especially likely to be observed in those living near the edge of death. So they gathered at the bedsides of the dying, to see what they might learn about the true meaning of life. Then they dedicated themselves to writing up the stories of their dying loved ones, struggling to account for the powerful emotions and lasting spiritual experiences they encountered there.

As Mrs. Hunter herself showed by her intensely introspective journaling, J. Wood demonstrated in his detailed account, and Dawn Moore made evident with her poignant eulogy: there is something powerful about putting into written words the stories of your loved ones' deaths. You don't have to be a beautiful writer—you don't have to be particularly eloquent or articulate. Still, as Dawn Moore and countless other eulogists have done, you can hand down to future generations what J. Wood called "a few words by way of elucidation."

4

CROWNED WITH THE DIVINE BLESSING: THE PARADOX OF DEATH

Mrs. Hunter was the daughter of the late Mr. Clulow, of Macclesfield. Her very pious and excellent mother was peculiarly attentive to her education, and laboured early in life to point out the way of salvation to her. This parental care was crowned with the divine blessing; the Lord, by a variety of means, drew her to himself, as appears from her own account.

— J. WOOD

To suggest that Donny Moore's tragic death from cancer was "happy" may sound ridiculous, even offensive, to the modern ear. This underscores the crucial challenge of "decoding" the language of early modern England to make sense of Mrs. Hunter's death.

As Mrs. Hunter and her peers used it, the word "happy" came from a very particular lineage. Specifically they inherited and embraced a strong cultural association of happiness with holiness of spirit, or purity of heart. This idea of "happy holiness"—or "holy happiness"—had evolved in England across the course of generations. The Old English word *hap* had referred to chance or good fortune. When, beginning in the fourteenth century, it began to be applied to an individual's demeanor, it was taken to mean "very glad." But the word carried with it strong connotations of the Roman Catholic concept of "beatification"—from the Latin *beatificare*—which was understood to mean "to make happy or make blessed." In the Roman Catholic Church, the first step toward canonization was for the person to be "beatified" or "pronounced as being in heavenly bliss." And in fact for generations Catholics in England and all of Europe had prayed for a happy death, associating this request especially with St. Joseph, asserted by tradition to have died in the presence of Jesus and Mary:

> Heavenly Father, when You are ready to lead me
> through death to eternal life, be with me as You were
> with Your people of old. As the last breath of life
> pours from me, take away all fear and let me em-
> brace You with joy. Give me the grace to die, as did
> St. Joseph, with Jesus and Mary at my side. Amen.

This perceived relationship between happiness, holiness, and the end of life was underscored in 1651 with the publication of Jeremy Taylor's twin books, *The Rule and Exercises of Holy Living* and *The Rule and Exercises of Holy Dying*. Taylor's books were dense works of "practical piety," linking the disciplined spiritual lives of the devout to the holiness of their deaths. In Taylor's view the truly faithful should spend their entire lives preparing to die so that when they died they might be spiritually prepared to live with God in eternity. Taylor's books remained among the most popular devotional tracts in England through the end of the eighteenth century; they were often published in fancy leather bindings usually reserved for the Bible itself. Whether or not Mrs. Hunter was personally familiar with "Taylor's Rules," she received as a part of her cultural inheritance his view that death was "so harmless a thing, that no good man was ever thought the more miserable for dying, but much the happier."

The idea that death can bring about a "happy ending" is in many ways a paradox, of course, but it is one intrinsic to the Christian tradition. The way the Bible tells the story, death on the cross represented for Jesus the culmination of his own personal religious quest, and the ultimate demonstration of the paradoxical spiritual truths he taught to his disciples: "the last shall be first and the first last" (Matthew 20:16); "greater love hath no man than this, than to lay down his life for his friends" (John 15:13); "for whosoever will save his life shall lose it, and whosoever will lose his life for my sake shall find it" (Matthew 16:25). Christians understand these paradoxical truths to have been confirmed in Jesus' death—celebrated on the paradoxically named "Good Friday"—as God used the cross for the purpose of saving humankind. For those who practice this ritualized way of dying, Christ's was the original and definitive "happy death."

The accounts of happy deaths published in the eighteenth and early nineteenth centuries reflect this paradoxical way of thinking throughout. Their authors did not deny that death brought pain and suffering. Still, they expected that this pain and suffering would be accompanied in equal measure by happiness and blessing, for both the dying and survivors alike. Because they had not been inculcated with the twentieth century's rationalist spirit, they lived comfortably with this and other paradoxes. Theirs was a worldview still primarily rooted in the Christian scriptures, and within this frame of reference it made perfect sense that young men and women would dedicate themselves to the pursuit of a happy death—after all, this is exactly what they believed their greatest hero had done.

This was the kind of death Mrs. Hunter was preparing to die in the months and years preceding January 1801: a death that would emulate Jesus' death; a death that would be fraught with such emotion it would lead others, paradoxically, to consider the abiding goodness of God.

My grandmother, Marian Smith, was born in 1910 in Howard, Kansas. She thought at an early age of becoming a foreign missionary, as did so many young women of her generation. Then one day it occurred to her that she could be a missionary right there in Kansas, and so that is what she has done with her life, dedicating herself to family and friends, neighbors and church, and cultivating a spiritual life grounded in simple devotions (morning and evening prayer, daily Bible reading, regular church attendance) and a life of service to others.

My earliest childhood memories are dominated by our family trips to my Grammy's house in El Dorado, Kansas. A simple, three-bedroom home with a gravel driveway and screened back porch, it was a common weekend destination for my parents, who lived in Kansas City when my brother and sisters and I were young. I still remember the excitement that came over me when our family car drove up that driveway—what a joy to arrive at a place so palpably filled with love.

At my grandmother's house my brother and sisters and cousins and I would ride in the back of our grandfather's pickup truck, explore the open alley out behind the house, and tiptoe barefoot around the metal grate that lay on the floor in the center of the living room, directly over the furnace burning in the basement. It seems ironic now, but that place—so filled with what today would be considered many dangers for small children—represents for me a place of supreme safety and security. It seems that way, of course, because of my grandmother, whose soft voice and serene demeanor could calm any childhood fear.

I remember the end of the day at my grandmother's house, when my siblings and cousins and I—all seven of us—would lie down on the floor in the living room with our blankets and sleeping bags. I remember the adults talking and laughing in the kitchen while we, the children, jabbered for a few minutes in the dark. Then my grandmother would come in. Kneeling on the floor beside us, starting with the smallest and working her way up the line, she would rub our backs and stroke our heads, whispering to us, putting us to sleep one by one. Sometimes now, when I am anxious and am having a hard time falling to sleep, I can still feel the hand of my grandmother on my back, so cool, so calming. I can still feel her hand on my head, fingers running through my hair. And I can still hear her voice, whispering softly in my ear.

When, as a young man, I returned to the religious faith of my ancestors, some of my sophisticated friends asked me, "Why?" I didn't have the guts to tell them—it sounds so supremely naive—but at the end of the day the honest answer to that question is "because my grandmother used to rub my back." I know exactly what J. Wood was talking about when he said of Mrs. Hunter's relationship with her mother, "this parental care was crowned with the divine blessing." Because my grandmother used to rub my back and place her hand on my head, I know that my life, too, has been touched by the hand of God.

While writing this book I had occasion to visit my grandmother; at the time of my visit she was ninety-four. Physically, my Grammy was profoundly limited. Her osteoporosis had rendered her stooped and able to walk only a few dozen steps at a time. Her sight was sufficiently limited by macular degeneration that she had to feel with her fork for bites of food on her plate—I cut the steak into bite-size pieces for her when she took me to dinner at the local steakhouse. And when she insisted on paying for our meal together, her hands were so weak I had to help her open and close the inner zipper on her purse.

Intellectually and spiritually, though, Grammy was a marvel. She said that people often asked her if her days weren't long—by that time her only trip out of the house most weeks was when friends picked her up to take her to church. She said she would tell them, "No, I can keep myself busy exploring my memories and imagination, and with the TV the whole world is available for me to consider." She persisted in a lifelong habit of recounting the ways in which she has been so blessed in this life—good family, warm bed, plenty to eat—and in reminding me of how many there are in this world "so much less fortunate than we are."

I found her persistent and determined cheerfulness almost maddening. There was a part of me that wanted her to share more openly with me the grief I knew she felt over the loss of so many things—her strength and mobility, her sight and the ability to travel to see family out of state, the lifelong friends whose deaths had resulted in her decades-old Bible study group "just sort of melting away." Not atypically for someone pushing ninety-five, she had outlived all the family of her generation, and all but one of her closest friends (and even this one would die just a few weeks after my visit).

And I wanted her to share more openly with me my own grief. We visited my grandfather's grave, but she was unable to walk the uneven lawn to his graveside, so I stood alone in the cold Kansas wind and counted the years she had survived him (almost twenty-five at the time of my visit). When I got back in the car I asked if she thought of him often. She said, "Oh, yes . . . every day"—and that was all.

Near the end of our visit I told her I missed her, and she said, "And I miss you, too, John," but then, unrelenting, added, "but I'm so glad we had this chance to visit." I wanted to grieve in anticipation that this might be the last time I would see her, but she would not have wanted to hear it—she said, instead, that she wanted me to bring my family with me "next time."

Of course a part of me can see at work in my grandmother the denial of death so pervasive in contemporary American culture. A part of me can also see at work in her a spirit of self-denial that was cultivated in women of her generation (and of many other generations, too), often to their own detriment. But I do not need to romanticize her to see at work in her another, more deeply held way of life.

At her kitchen table she asked if I knew the poem "Unweaponed Peace." "No, I don't," I said, and so she got out a book entitled *Kansas Fifth*—it was a "reader," a collection of poems and stories and songs.

"I don't believe they have these in school anymore," she said.

"I know they don't," I replied.

"I learned this poem first in fifth grade, but not much time ever passes before I find myself going back to it."

I read:

UNWEAPONED PEACE

John Greenleaf Whittier (1807–1892)

> *There is a story told*
> *In Eastern tents, when autumn nights grow cold,*
> *And round the fire the Mongol shepherds sit*
> *With grave responses listening unto it:*
> *Once, on the errands of his mercy bent,*
> *Buddha, the holy and benevolent,*
> *Met a fell monster, huge and fierce of look,*
> *Whose awful voice the hills and forests shook.*
> *"O Son of peace!" the giant cried, "thy fate*
> *Is sealed at last, and love shall yield to hate."*
> *The unarmed Buddha, looking, with no trace*
> *Of fear or anger, in the monster's face,*
> *In pity said: "Poor fiend, even thee I love."*
> *Lo! As he spake, the sky-tall terror sank*
> *To hand-breadth size; the huge abhorrence shrank*
> *Into the form and fashion of a dove;*
> *And where the thunder of its rage was heard*
> *Circling above him sweetly sang the bird;*
> *"Hate hath no harm for love"—so ran the song;*
> *"And peace unweaponed conquers every wrong."*

I imagined what an exciting and exotic thing it must have been for my grandmother to embrace this poem while growing up in a small town in Kansas. I thought how radical her faith must have been in her day, to embrace a lesson attributed to an "unarmed Buddha." The sentiment expressed in this late-nineteenth-century poem did not surprise me, though, for I heard in it an echo from the eighteenth century and beyond, the echo of a faith that would cast matters of the spirit in paradoxical juxtaposition with one another.

My grandmother's spirit is of this paradoxical sort. It makes sense, in this spirit, to think that love can conquer hate, to expect power to come from weakness, to find unspeakable joy in the midst of grief. It makes sense, in this spirit, to seek a "happy death," and it was clear to me as I visited with her that my grandmother was preparing herself for this practice. As the unarmed Buddha said to the "fell monster, huge and fierce of look," so my grandmother is prepared to say to death, "Poor fiend, even thee I love." In the language of the liturgy that will be spoken at her funeral, she is "living as one who is unafraid to die." I have no doubt that my grandmother, when her time comes, will die "as one who goes forth to live."

I left my grandmother's house at 5 A.M. the next day, needing to drive an hour to catch an early plane. My Grammy got up with me, not for breakfast, but to pray. Sitting in her kitchen, we took each other's hands. I told her I loved her and I thanked her for loving me the way she has. "I've counted on it," I said. Without responding directly to me, my Grammy started to pray, deflecting the praise: "Thank you, God, for your most wonderful and unbelievable love, which is with us always. Help us to love you by serving others, that we may know your peace."

I said a prayer myself, and then we prayed the Lord's Prayer together, and then it was done.

I kneeled by her chair and gave her a hug. We said our good-byes and our "I love you"s and I picked up my bags and walked out the door. I walked to the car and as I climbed in and started the engine, I was overcome with emotion. More accurately, I was overcome with mixed emotions. On the one hand, I was overcome by sadness, in anticipated grief, thinking, "this may well be the last time I see my grandmother." But I also found myself overcome by joy, trying to think if there had ever been a time I had felt this happy. I was so happy . . . so happy to have been sent on my way in this life by one who is so happy herself.

It was cold and dark as I drove away from my grandmother—Marian Alice Sliker Smith, in her ninety-fifth year of life. I turned east onto the highway and toward the rising sun.

5

SURE OF GOING TO HEAVEN:
LOVE LIKE AN OCEAN

When about seven years of age, I frequently got Janeway's Token for Children, *went into a room, and read it by myself: I then prayed that God would make me as happy as those little children of whom I had read, and as sure of going to heaven as they were. One time when I had been reading and praying over that little book, as I was coming out of the room it was impressed on my mind to turn back and pray again. I thought I have prayed once, that is enough, and took hold of the door to come out; but the impression to return and pray again, was so strong that I obeyed the call, and was filled with such happiness that I thought, if I then died, I was sure of going to heaven.*

—— FROM MRS. HUNTER'S JOURNAL

Go into any bookstore and you'll see that the section labeled "spirituality" consumes considerable shelf space, a simple indicator that the topic of the afterlife never ceases to engage

our imaginations. The questions these books attempt to answer are as old as religion itself. Is there such a thing as the
human "soul," something that exists apart from our physically grounded consciousness? If so, is there a God waiting
to receive our souls on the other side of death? What kind of
reception will it be? As the old saying goes, there is nothing
like death to focus the mind on God.

As strange as it may seem, thoughts like these were for Mary
Clulow the stuff of everyday life. Born in 1775 she, like all
children of her generation, would have been steeped in talk of
dying, and encouraged to confront the prospect of her own
death at the earliest imaginable age. The only reason she could
read, for instance, was because she had learned the alphabet by
practicing rhymes like these: "G: As runs the *Glass* / Man's life
doth pass"; "T: *Time* cuts down all / both great and small";
"X: *Xerxes* the great did die / And so must you and I"; "Y:
Youth forward slips / Death soonest nips." And it is almost
certain that at bedtime she prayed the familiar age-old prayer:

> *Now I lay me down to sleep,*
> *I pray the Lord my soul to keep.*
> *And should I die before I wake,*
> *I pray the Lord my soul to take. Amen.*

One day in prayer, the seven-year-old Mary Clulow experienced an overwhelming sensation of happiness—though not
the kind we talk about today, derived from the satisfaction of
wants and desires. The happiness she experienced that day was
akin to holiness, a peace of soul derived from mystical communion with God in the present life and an inner confidence
that all will be well in the next. In a moment of transcendent

spiritual experience, she understood herself to be among a select group of children—those who were "sure of going to heaven."

———

Mary Clulow was far from unique among eighteenth-century children in her experience of spiritual awakening, nor was she alone in associating it with the book called *Janeway's Token for Children*. Authored by James Janeway, and consisting entirely of stories of children who died and went to heaven, the book was formally entitled *A Token for Children: Being an Exact Assessment of the Conversion, Holy and Exemplary Lives, and Joyful Deaths of Several Young Children*. In all probability Mary Clulow received her copy of *Janeway's Token* from an older sibling, or from another child in her church or neighborhood. In part because of its popularity as a "hand-me-down," *Janeway's Token* was among the most widely read children's books for generations in both England and America, as prominent in the imaginations of Puritan and Protestant households as the works of Dr. Seuss are today.

To us all this seems bizarre—almost macabre—but it made sense in light of death's imposing presence in Mrs. Hunter's day. As did many other publications, the New York–based *Daily Christian Advocate* published a weekly log of deaths of its readership in the area. Just one, selected randomly in my browsing from the early nineteenth century, gives a feel for the devastating distribution of death across the life span:

> The City Inspector reports the death of 107 persons during the week ending on Saturday the 23 . . . 21 men, 25 women, 34 boys and 27 girls. Of whom:

26 were of or under the age of I year,

19 between I and 2,

8 between 2 and 5,

3 between 5 and I0,

5 between I0 and 20,

I0 between 20 and 30,

I5 between 30 and 40,

7 between 40 and 50,

4 between 50 and 60,

6 between 60 and 70,

3 between 70 and 80, and

I between 80 and 90.

Faced with a reality like this, it made perfect sense that small children like Mary Clulow should begin their spiritual preparations for death. Poring through the latest volume of *Janeway's Token,* Mary Clulow was beginning to form a vision of herself, a vision that would be fulfilled in the life of J. Wood's "Mrs. Hunter." She was beginning to imagine herself as the kind of person who could die a happy death.

The religious doctrine that undergirded the hope of heaven— and fueled the popularity of publications like *Janeway's Token*—went by the name of "assurance," an understanding that by an inner witness of the Spirit ordinary Christians could be assured of their eternal salvation. This idea was hotly disputed in Mrs. Hunter's day, and had been for centuries. While all Christians believed quite viscerally in the reality of heaven and hell, and understood the moment of dying to be a moment in which every person would face God's judgment, the doctrine of assurance—the idea that one could be *confident* of going to heaven—ran a fault line through the Protestant movements on the European continent and their Puritan counterparts in England and America.

In the majority view—associated with John Calvin, the Swiss reformer whose fundamental theological principle was the absolute sovereignty of God—the eternal state of the individual soul could not be known from this side of the veil of death. Believing God's judgments in these matters to be utterly inscrutable, "Calvinists" promoted a humble and penitent spiritual posture in the face of death. The truly faithful would approach the end of their lives with a spirit of "fear and trembling," praying traditional deathbed prayers of confession.

Standing against the Calvinists were Protestants and Puritans influenced by the Dutch theologian Jacob Arminius, who lived and taught in the late sixteenth century. Arminius believed the faithful could become consciously aware of God's grace and were capable of cooperating with it. So the "Arminianists" in the seventeenth and eighteenth centuries aspired to a kind of spiritual confidence that struck a sharp contrast to the Calvinists' penitential posture. For people persuaded by the Arminian impulse an assurance of salvation—especially as this could be demonstrated in the face of death—was the hallmark of fully realized faith.

By the turn of the eighteenth century the tension between Calvinism and Arminianism could be found within virtually every church on both sides of the Atlantic—and indeed within every Protestant and Puritan soul. Preachers and parishioners alike swung wildly back and forth along a spectrum defined by the poles of God's sovereignty and God's grace. Calvinists sought to protect the judgment and righteousness of a perfectly sovereign God; salvation would be received as an entirely unmerited gift by a secret company of the elect. Arminianists emphasized that grace was the very essence of God's nature; salvation was a gift, to be sure, but one offered to, and within the reach of, every faithful man, woman, and child.

The rise of Methodism—a movement of renewal in the eighteenth-century Church of England—parallels precisely the spread of the doctrine of assurance. That Methodists prided themselves on this association is evidenced in the title they chose for their movement's bimonthly publication, *The Arminian*, and in the journal entries of countless Methodist preachers. Methodists were by no means the only Christians to die happy deaths in early modern England and America, but they embraced the ritual with particular fervor. A happy death seemed the perfect expression of their optimistic spirituality: what better way to demonstrate confidence in God's grace than to approach the moment of judgment with a spirit of happiness and in a posture of praise?

And so, as they lived their holy lives and died their happy deaths, Methodists taught their children what they considered to be life's most important lesson: nothing—not even death itself—would be able to separate them from the love of God.

When I began my work as a pastor, I was unprepared to answer questions about the nature of life beyond death. In my late twenties when I was ordained, I was unconcerned with death even as I embarked upon a career that would force me to confront it so directly. I was more concerned at that time in my life with the "here-and-now" dimensions of the religious life. I was committed to peace and social justice and right relationships among the living. I professed disdain for preachers of "pie-in-the-sky" salvation and heard in their promises a temptation to avoid confronting what were for me the more urgent demands of faith: to seek justice, love kindness, and walk humbly in this life with God and neighbor.

My cultivated ignorance in questions of the afterlife came crashing in on me one day in 1997, when I received a call from one of my parishioners, Laura Dawson, who asked me if I would pay a visit to her seven-year-old grandson, Jason, in the hospital. Expecting to hear that he had suffered some kind of accident, I said, "of course," and then asked why he had been hospitalized. "He is dying of cancer," she said. My heart dropped. I asked for directions to the hospital and said I would be there in a few hours.

I remember driving to the hospital that day and being overwhelmed at the thought of having to look Jason's parents in the eye. Three years earlier my wife, Jennifer, and I had adopted an infant girl, bringing resolution to our years-long battle with infertility. I remember thinking of my daughter, Ellen, with whom I was so desperately in love, and trying to imagine what it would be like for me and Jennifer if Ellen, not a little boy named Jason, lay dying in a hospital bed. I remember pulling into the hospital parking lot and burying my head in the steering wheel, sobbing. I found myself crying for so many reasons I couldn't untangle them all. I was crying for Jason, and for his parents. But I was also crying for my wife and my daughter, the losses in their lives (the dream of a biological child, the relationship with a biological mother) somehow mysteriously mingled with the impending death of a little boy I had never met. I was also crying for myself, unconvinced that I would be able to shed my own emotional baggage in this new pastoral assignment. Years later, when I came across the accounts of happy dying from the turn of the nineteenth century, I would remember vividly the day I sat sobbing uncontrollably in the hospital parking lot. Again and again in the accounts of happy deaths, visitors at the deathbeds of the dying are reported to have been "greatly affected," a common outcome of which was to burst out in tears.

I honestly do not remember a thing about that visit, my first, with Jason Robb and his parents, Barry and Niki. I remember my parishioner Laura, Niki's mother, greeting me in the waiting room outside the children's cancer wing, and I remember her showing me a picture of Jason from the year before—he was smiling a gap-toothed grin, and he had a full head of curls, sun-bleached blond from hours at the beach, which she told me was his favorite place in the world. And I remember following a nurse in a flower-print hospital shirt to the bed. But I do not remember what we talked about, Jason's parents and I. I'm sure I asked them for a description of Jason's condition, and I'm sure I mostly listened, because I know I felt ill equipped to offer much in the way of "wisdom." I do not remember what I said, or what I prayed, or even whether I prayed. Looking back on it, I realize I do not remember because I was in shock.

Within a day or two I was back at the hospital, again at Laura's request. This time she had asked me to come for a specific reason, to discuss with Barry and Niki the idea of having their son baptized. Jason's doctors had abandoned any hope of a cure, and the hospital staff was now dedicated to offering him and his family physical comfort and emotional support.

Spiritual guidance was also called for, of course, but, again, I was unsure whether I was suited for the task.

I was unsure in part because Barry and Niki had not been to church in years and I saw in them so much of my generation's ambivalence toward "organized religion." Niki had remained almost entirely silent during my first visit—I had spoken almost entirely with Barry—and while it seemed probable that this was simply the result of her grief and shock, I knew it was entirely possible that she felt ambivalent about the church. Who in my generation didn't? And I couldn't pretend her ambivalence was ill considered or illegitimate. I worked in the church and knew firsthand its many failings and limitations.

I suspected that Jason's grandmother Laura was the one pushing the idea of baptism and was not convinced that this was Barry's and Niki's deep desire. Did the church—the stubborn, stuffy, so often judgmental and antiquated church—have anything to say to the parents of a seven-year-old boy whose body was wasting away before their eyes? What difference could a mere formality like baptism make in Jason's life when he was about to die? I don't know for certain if these questions were on his parents' minds, but I knew they were running through my own as I drove to my second visit with Jason Robb. I was not convinced I knew the answers to these questions, nor what I would want to hear if I were in their position and an unfamiliar pastor came to visit my dying child.

I don't know how we got onto the topic, but in my second visit Jason's parents and I ended up talking about how much he loved going to the beach. I remember talking about sunburns and sand castles and seashells, and I remember for one brief moment feeling like I was talking to them at a backyard barbecue, instead of at the foot of a hospital bed. I remember laughing with them about how sandy children can get at the beach and what a hassle it can be to try to keep their hands free of sand while they eat their snacks. I remember being shocked at how easily the laughter came, it seeming on the one hand inappropriate and on the other entirely apt.

When the question of baptism came up, Niki said, "I wish we could do it in the ocean" and for the first time allowed herself to cry in my presence. I cried, too, and then said, "Why don't I bring the ocean to Jason?"

At my third visit I baptized Jason with water scooped into a plastic bucket from the Pacific Ocean off the shores of Redondo Beach. At the hospital, unconvinced I knew what I was doing, I clung to the baptismal liturgy as if to a sailboat mast in a stormy sea:

Eternal God, your mighty acts of salvation have
been made known through water—from the
moving of your Spirit upon the waters of creation,
to the deliverance of your people through the flood
and through the Red Sea.
In the fullness of time you sent Jesus, nurtured
in the water of a womb, baptized by John, and
anointed by your Spirit.
He called his disciples to share in the baptism
of his death and resurrection and to make
disciples of all nations.
Pour out your Holy Spirit to bless this gift of water
and this child who receives it, to wash away his sin and
clothe him in righteousness throughout his life, that,
dying and being raised with Christ, he may share in his
final victory; through the same Jesus Christ our Lord.

And with that I poured water over Jason's head—shorn by chemotherapy of what were once long blond curls—and said, "Jason Donald, I baptize you in the name of the Father, and of the Son, and of the Holy Spirit." He died just a few hours later.

Six days after his death we gathered for Jason's funeral at his grandparents' church. Word of the funeral had been communicated to the family's friends and to the staff and families at Jason's school, and the sanctuary was packed. The invitation had included the request to bring seashells—an ancient symbol of Christian baptism.

Near the start of the funeral I invited the children to come to the front of the sanctuary for a "time with children," a familiar ritual on Sunday mornings in most mainline Protestant churches. Instead of the dozen or fifteen children that I was used to seeing on Sunday mornings, though, at Jason's funeral there were almost one hundred children sitting on the chancel steps. I asked them how many liked to go to the beach and of course they all raised their hands. I asked what they liked to do at the beach and they shouted out predictable answers—"make sand castles," "bodysurf," "get sandy," "lie in the sun." I then asked them if they had ever really looked at the sand from the beach:

> Have you ever really looked at the sand at the beach? I have, and you know what? At first it seems like all the grains of sand are the same, but if you really look closely you can see that they're not. Each of them is different—different colors, different shapes. And a lot of them, if you look at them real close, you can tell are really not grains of sand at all. Really they are little, tiny

pieces of seashells. You know how seashells get washed up and down on the beach? And you know how they get broken up as the waves push them all around? Well, it turns out when you look at the beach, when you look at a handful of sand, you can't always tell what are the grains of sand and what are the little pieces of seashell. You can tell the bigger pieces of seashell. But the longer they are on the seashore, the more the seashells get broken into littler and littler pieces.

I know you are very, very sad about your friend Jason. And I know some of you are wondering what is going to happen to him, now that he is dead. In churches like this one we talk about going to heaven, and that's where we believe Jason is right now. But "heaven" is sort of hard to get a picture of—and it's hard because no one really knows what it looks like, or even where it is. So today let's pretend that heaven is like a big beach, a beach with a big ocean washing up on the shore.

I believe that heaven is sort of like that beach, and I believe that God is sort of like that ocean. The beach is a part of the ocean, and the ocean is a part of the beach. And there are more seashells than you can count in that ocean, and more than you can count on the beach. Some of them are whole—some are big and some are small, some have animals living in them and some don't—and they are easy to see because they really still look like shells. But some other shells aren't easy to see, because they've been broken into little pieces. But they are still there. They are still a part of the beach, and they are still a part of the ocean.

I believe Jason is a part of that beach called "heaven" and a part of that ocean called "God." Just a few days ago I got to baptize Jason—that's something we pastors get to do. We get to put water on people's heads and remind them that they are children of God. When I baptized Jason I got to tell him that God loved him, and would always love him, and I got to tell him that he would never be far from God. I believe that about Jason—that God loves him more than words can tell, and that he will never be far from God. I believe that about you, too, and I am so glad you came here today.

I had purchased a large glass vase for the occasion and filled the bottom with sand from the beach where Jason's baptismal water had been drawn. I asked the children to put their seashells in the vase and I held my microphone by the vase as they dropped them in. The clatter was like bells ringing gently, the shells striking different notes as the vase filled up. I am reminded now of the seventeenth-century Puritan poet Anne Bradstreet, who described life as beautiful, but fragile—"like as a bubble, or brittle glass."

Of course Jason Robb's death cannot be thought of as "happy" in the simple, modern sense of the term. Not a single person was happy that cancer had called them to church that day to memorialize a seven-year-old boy. But many, many people said to me on the way out of Jason's funeral, "Thank you for that wonderful service," or "I am so glad my little girl got to be here today." And no words will ever mean more to me than the ones Jason's father spoke to me: "Thank you for your compassion."

Jason's funeral was the occasion of great healing and great happiness, not because I did such a wonderful job of it, but because the reality of a little boy's death brought many, many people to consider the abundant beauty of this life and to experience at least a taste of the transcendent goodness of God. People left Jason's funeral sure that he was going to heaven, and hopeful that they would be, too.

A shocking number of the published accounts from the eighteenth and nineteenth centuries chronicle the deaths of children, youths, and young adults. Mrs. Hunter, who died at twenty-six, was in no way considered unusually young to die. This also helps to explain the pathos in which accounts of dying children were drenched. Their authors did not mean to make light of the deaths of the children, who died so often and so young. They were written by parents and pastors hoping to share with others what they had learned from the deaths of their young people about God's larger ways of working in the world.

That these deaths were considered "happy" did not refer merely—or even primarily—to the dying person's subjective emotional state. "Happy" was a more comprehensive term than that, referring to the universal (indeed cosmic) circumstances of the person's dying. In truly happy deaths, those who were dying were assured of their own salvation. In happy deaths the dying persons' spiritual mentors were made proud of them and found new evidence with which to encourage others in their family or church. In happy deaths family and friends were comforted and reassured—of their loved one's eternal well-being, of their own prospects of salvation, and of the triumphant goodness of God. In happy deaths others were encouraged—through exhortation, encouragement, and calls to repentance—to "work out their own salvation." For its practitioners, the ritual of the happy death witnessed to the goodness of God, not just in the present, and not just for the person dying, but indeed for all of time and for all of humankind. In a happy death God was well served and well represented and well pleased.

Seven years after Jason Robb died I telephoned his parents, who had moved to northern California, to tell them I was writing up the story of Jason's death and funeral. Niki picked up the phone and greeted me with a warmth and enthusiasm I had not heard seven years before.

She reminded me she had been seven months' pregnant when Jason died—something I had completely forgotten—and she described for me the birth of her daughter, Alyssa: "After Jason died I took a disability leave from work, because I just wasn't able to focus on anything. But then Alyssa came along, and forced me to focus . . . you know, the way babies do. There were things that just had to be done. And she was such a good baby, and she is so wonderful, and so full of life. It really was a blessing. It still is."

I could hear Alyssa in the background over the phone—talking to her older sister, who was five at the time of Jason's death and had now just turned thirteen. Alyssa would have just turned seven, the same age Jason was when he died; the same age Mary Hunter was when she had her spiritual awakening while reading *Janeway's Token for Children*. Talking with Niki on the phone that day, I couldn't help but form a picture of Alyssa in my mind. Surely she has big blond curls, I thought, like her brother Jason, whom she never met. And surely she has a smile like his, and a love of the beach. And surely she has a share in his baptism, a share in Jesus' life and death—in "the baptism of his suffering, death and resurrection," as the church's historic liturgy puts it.

Surely Alyssa is going to heaven, I thought to myself, following in the footsteps of her brother Jason.

And she is, isn't she?

6

THE WHOLE HEART:
ON EARTH AS IT IS IN HEAVEN

When I was about eighteen years and four months old, I saw clearly,
that unless my sins were forgiven me, I could not go to heaven. I
then began to seek the Lord with my whole heart. For one month I
was in deep distress, but at length proved the faithful promise verified,
"Ye shall seek me, and find me, when ye shall search for me with all
your heart."

— FROM MRS. HUNTER'S JOURNAL

Most modern people tend to think of religion as, primarily,
a matter of belief. When new acquaintances learn that I am a
pastor, many turn tail and flee, fearful that I will try to talk
them into believing things they don't want to believe. Even
those who are not awkward about the subject of religion betray
with their questions the common assumption that faith can be
boiled down to questions of belief. "What do people in your

church believe about this?" they ask. "What do they believe about that?"

Mrs. Hunter and her peers in the late eighteenth century did not consider questions of religious belief unimportant, but their primary concern was not that they get things right intellectually. For them the life of faith was more about the heart than it was about the head. So Mary Clulow—not yet married and just a few months past her eighteenth birthday— saw clearly what should be her life's principal ambition: to love God with her whole heart.

The scripture that she recorded in her journal was from the book of Jeremiah—"Ye shall seek me, and find me, when ye shall search for me with all your heart"—but the prophet was referencing the famous first commandment of the Hebrew Bible, as found in the book of Deuteronomy—"thou shalt love the Lord thy God with all thine heart, and with all thy soul, and with all thy might." According to the Christian gospels, Jesus called this "the greatest commandment," and coupled it with one that "is like unto it, thou shalt love thy neighbour as thyself." He taught his disciples: "On these two command- ments hang all the law and the prophets" (Matthew 22:39–40, referencing Leviticus 19:18).

People in Mrs. Hunter's day believed there was a name for the spiritual condition prescribed by the Bible's greatest commandment—they called it "holiness." As Methodism's founder, John Wesley, had defined it, holiness consisted of "salvation from all sin, and loving God with an undivided heart." This shorthand definition encompassed the two great prongs of Reformation theology: "justification," by which God was understood to justify individual believers, forgiving their sin; and "sanctification," by which God was perceived to make the faithful more and more sanctified, or holy.

For Wesley holiness was not a static spiritual condition but a "habitual inclination" that could be cultivated intentionally by every ordinary Christian. The defining characteristics of this way of life were simple: "humility, faith, hope and love," as he named them in one of his own favorite sermons, called "The Circumcision of the Heart." The last of these was most fundamental:

> Love is the first and greatest commandment, and love combines all the commandments into one . . . The royal law of heaven and earth is this: "You shall love the Lord your God with all your heart, and with all your soul, and with all your mind, and with all your strength."

Wesley claimed this doctrine of holiness as his movement's unique contribution to eighteenth-century Christendom. He and his followers exhorted every ordinary Christian to "work out your own salvation," conveniently dropping from their exhortations the familiar clause "with fear and trembling" that completed the quotation from Philippians 2:12 and made the scripture sound insufficiently hopeful—and altogether too Calvinistic—to their Arminianist ears.

Wesley also embraced the understanding that devotion to God should provoke a passionate commitment to the poor and lost of the world. This understanding, which recurs again and again in the great monastic traditions of Christianity, had been largely lost in the ceremonialism of the Anglican tradition of the seventeenth and eighteenth centuries. Claiming that "all religion is social religion" and subjecting himself knowingly to the Protestant charge of "works righteousness," Wesley called on his followers to be zealous in their pursuit of good works.

Mary Clulow Hunter, an exemplary Methodist, was extraordinarily busy in "working out her own salvation." She was busy at worship and prayer, busy at reading the Bible, busy at doing good. She did not perceive her life to be divided into spheres—"private" and "public," "work" and "play," "personal" and "social"—as so many modern people are inclined to do. The whole of her life was consumed with her search for holiness, or "purity of heart." She perceived her every act—from "attending to her little ones" to "visiting persons in the sick-ward," from "domestic duties" to her dedicated times of prayer—as a part of this single, overriding concern. For Mrs. Hunter the life of faith was by no means confined to church—to the contrary, she saw opportunities to exercise holiness at every turn and in every avenue of life. She dedicated her daily living to fulfilling the most familiar phrase from Jesus' most familiar prayer: "Thy kingdom come, thy will be done, on earth as it is in heaven."

To the modern mind, accustomed to distinguishing between the "religious" and "secular" parts of life, all this may seem strange, even fanatical. And it is hard for contemporary people—even those who identify strongly with their religious tradition—to imagine that a life of such all-consuming focus could be experienced as anything but oppressive. According to her journal, though, Mrs. Hunter did not experience her single-minded and single-hearted devotion as a burden. Rather, it brought her great joy. As J. Wood summarized a typical season in her life of faith: "In the Spring following she was much indisposed, but was very happy, as will appear from her own words."

In the summer of 1992, straight out of seminary, I became the pastor of a tiny United Methodist church in Calexico, California. A city of twenty thousand located two hours east of San Diego on the U.S.–Mexican border, Calexico is the poorest city in Imperial County, itself among the poorest counties in California. It is also situated below sea level in the heart of the Imperial Valley desert; for over seven months each year, the average daily high exceeds 100 degrees. It is, for a great many reasons, a difficult place to live.

Nancy Martens was one of the first people I met in Calexico. A few days after my arrival she left a round tin container of chocolate fudge on the front doorstep of my house, along with a note welcoming me and my family to town. And on my first Sunday at church I found her in the sanctuary early, before the start of worship, preparing the bread and juice for communion.

Barely five feet tall, Nancy had short-cropped gray-blond hair and a face that only looked wrinkled on the rare occasion it did not feature a smile. Her style of dress was simple, her blue windbreaker well weathered and worn. Though I knew nothing of her politics, she reminded me of the older women my friends in the 1980s Central American solidarity movement affectionately called "little old ladies for peace in tennis shoes." I liked her instantly.

Nancy was born in Wisconsin but moved to Calexico in

1946, when she married John Martens, a Calexico native. John was the son of some of Calexico's original European settlers, Swiss-Italian and German immigrants who moved into the Imperial Valley at the turn of the twentieth century and built the massive canals that turned the desert lowlands into spectacularly fertile farms.

Early each morning since her arrival in Calexico, Nancy Martens had walked the city's streets, a ritual affording her some good exercise and the chance to thank God for the new day. In her almost fifty years of morning walks she had watched her adopted hometown undergo a remarkable transformation.

When Nancy had arrived in the Imperial Valley at the end of World War II, it was still a small farming enclave whose residents were predominantly of European ancestry. By the time I arrived in 1992, the valley was a different place altogether. The population was predominantly Mexican and Mexican-American. The farmlands had been consolidated time and time again. The economy cycled mercilessly with the seasons of the year and the international price of crops like carrots, lettuce, onions, and beets.

This economic and demographic transformation was most dramatic in Calexico, the Imperial Valley's border town. By 1990, 98 percent of Calexico's residents were of Mexican ancestry. The seasonal unemployment rate ran as high as 40 percent. Its local merchants had become entirely dependent on cross-border traffic from Mexicali, the city growing explosively on the other side of the border. Calexico had become the northernmost suburb of a massive Mexican city. It was, in effect, a Mexican town that just happened to be located in the United States.

The vast majority of Calexico's Anglo residents had dealt with these changes, quite simply, by relocating. Some stayed in the Imperial Valley but moved to towns farther from the border; a great many left the valley altogether. A small number stayed in Calexico, grumbling. An even smaller number, Nancy Martens among them, stayed in Calexico and just kept smiling.

A principal focus of Nancy's life in Calexico was her participation in the women's group at her church. In United Methodist churches this group is called United Methodist Women (UMW). Like the women's associations in most mainline Protestant churches, Calexico's women's organization was long past its organizational prime, and it was plagued by a scarcity of able-bodied workers for the many tasks and responsibilities that had accumulated across decades of faithful service. By the time I arrived as the pastor of the church in 1992, the enormous demographic transitions had reduced Calexico's UMW to just fifteen members. Their diminished numbers notwithstanding, Calexico's women still found ways to accomplish together a bewildering assortment of good works—from feeding the hungry, to hosting church rummage sales, to staffing the board of a local church-related social services agency, to caring for the sick and dying, to funding missionaries abroad. While naturally possessing all the frailties of the human condition, and lost at times in the midst of sea changes in the culture around them, the members of this women's organization were the backbone of the church, as is the case at so many churches belonging to "old-line" Protestant denominations.

As was typical for women belonging to church organizations like United Methodist Women, Nancy Martens was famous in Calexico for feeding people. For decades she had prepared communion at the Methodist church and managed the kitchen for all-church potlucks. She also routinely took meals to the sick and dying and volunteered in the free lunch program for low-income seniors at the community center downtown. She regularly hosted church gatherings at her home and delivered goodies to the sick and the shut-in while making her morning rounds on foot. Mine was by no means the first family to receive baked goods from Nancy Martens. Every day she took her morning walk, leaving behind a trail of strategically placed plastic baggies and cookie tins and Tupperware containers.

About a year into my stay I came across Nancy during one of her morning walks and found her feeding a notoriously aggressive neighborhood dog. I laughed and asked her if she knew this dog well.

"Oh yes," she said, and pulled a half dozen doggie treats out of the pocket of her windbreaker. And then, with a smile and a giggle, she said, "I have a great many friends in this town."

By that time I knew enough about Calexico to understand a little bit about how things had come to be the way they were. The combination of poverty and cross-border traffic had made crime a chronic problem, an unexpected consequence of which was that a great many of the city's residents kept aggressive guard dogs in their yards for protection. Nancy had adapted to this change as she had adapted to so many other changes in her life, by befriending and embracing what others dreaded and feared.

In 1994 Nancy was diagnosed with an untreatable cancer, and she promptly went about the business of preparing for her death. Her top priority was teaching her husband, John, how to cook.

John Martens was, by his own assessment, "an ornery old cuss." More than a foot taller than Nancy, John was, depending on how you looked at it, a complementary or contrasting partner for his wife of fifty-five years. He was an archconservative, she a lifelong liberal. He had sworn off religion in his youth; she was a devout churchgoer. John was darkness and pessimism and grumbling. Nancy was sunshine and hope and light.

Unlike Nancy, John had not adapted so gracefully to the changes in his hometown. He often lamented the state of affairs in Calexico and the neighboring towns on the U.S. side of the border, and he couldn't stop himself from reminiscing about—and romanticizing—the past.

John was not a racist, but he did resent the fact that the rise of Mexican culture in Calexico had virtually erased the legacy of his Swiss-German ancestors. Still, he prided himself on his fluency in Spanish. We would often exchange pleasantries in Spanish, and throughout my time in Calexico he called me "Padre," taking delight in the irony of that designation for someone almost fifty years his junior.

When I visited with John on his own, as I had a number of occasions to do in Nancy's dying weeks, he never failed to sing his wife's praises and wonder out loud what he was going to do after her death. He also questioned me persistently, asking how I could believe in a God who would take someone like "dear, dear Nancy" and leave behind a no-good louse like himself.

Like many couples of their generation, John and Nancy had cultivated a stark and absolute division of household labor. John, who had worked for years as a general contractor, was responsible for the outside of the house; Nancy was responsible for the inside. Nancy cooked; John ate. John had been happy to benefit all these years from Nancy's passion for food, and he quite literally did not know his way around the kitchen.

And so, in the three months that passed between her decision to forgo radical chemotherapy and her death, Nancy taught her husband how to cook. She put labels on the kitchen cupboards and drawers. She took him shopping and showed him around the grocery store. She culled from her files the recipes she was confident John would be able to prepare, and, while John looked on, she prepared these dishes to demonstrate.

Nancy fell into a coma for several days before she died, but a few days prior to that she invited me to stop by for the women's circle meeting she would be hosting at her home.

"Are you sure you are up to that?" I asked.

"Oh yes," Nancy replied. "John has promised to help."

That Thursday morning I got to Nancy's house about 10 A.M. Her hospital bed was in the living room, and her friends were seated in chairs scattered around the room. Nancy was sitting up in her bed and smiling. She looked frail and weak, but her smile was the same as it had been every other time I'd seen her. As I moved across the room to greet her, I saw that she had a tray on her lap and on it was a tea service, complete with saucers and cups. It dawned on me that Nancy Martens was sitting up in her deathbed and serving tea to her friends.

Even more remarkable was how I found John. John was working the room with a tray in his hand, passing out cookies and pastries.

"Would you like a muffin, Padre?" he asked.

I didn't know whether to laugh or cry.

Nancy Martens's funeral was one of the first I ever officiated. She was one of the first people to invite me, as a pastor, to join her on her journey to death. Now, looking back on it, I can see what a remarkable journey it was. Nancy was one of those rare people who was exactly the same person in every sphere of her life—at work in play and playful at work; at home in the world and welcoming the world into her home. A spiritual virtuoso, she succeeded in cultivating the deeply held habit of loving God continually, with an undivided heart.

So it was that Nancy Martens was genuinely unfazed by the spiritual work of dying. More than that, she was genuinely contented as she died. Nancy did not just accept death—she embraced it as she embraced the other dramatic changes in her life, from a spiritual posture of openness and trust. Because there were not, in her way of thinking about things, two distinct places called "heaven" and "earth," she died the very same way she lived, a happy woman.

In my subsequent years of working with the aged and dying, I would become familiar with the stock phrases that people of Nancy's generation commonly use as they confront the reality of death. "I've had a good life." "I never thought I'd live this long to begin with." "There are so many people less fortunate than myself."

But there is great variability in the spirit with which people share these ritualized expressions. Many express them as if they are the crowning arguments in an ongoing debate, a debate they are not convinced they will really win.

Nancy Martens expressed these sentiments with a tone of sheer gratitude. She smiled as she spoke these words. She smiled as she looked back on her life, and she smiled as she talked about going to heaven. The way Nancy Martens thought about it, the dimension of the here and now and the dimension of the hereafter were cut from the same cloth, the cloth of God's inexhaustible love.

A few months later John told me that Nancy's smile was the last thing he remembered of her in the moments before she died.

7

IN THE HANDS OF GOD:

ENTRE TUS MANOS, SEÑOR

Betwixt five and six weeks after I found peace, the Lord was pleased to take my dear mother to himself. Before her death she looked at me, and said, "I am going to leave thee, Mary, in a troublesome world, fatherless and motherless; but I leave thee in the hands of God."

—— FROM MRS. HUNTER'S JOURNAL

Just a few weeks after she found peace with God, the eighteen-year-old Mary Clulow said farewell to her dying mother. If she needed confirmation that her life was in God's hands, she got it, verbatim, in her mother's deathbed blessing.

The spiritual posture adopted by the young Mary Clulow's mother is easily confused with what we today call "letting go." This language betrays, though, our modern worldview—believing the world to consist of many "things" that are available to be "possessed," we suddenly, as death comes into view, perceive the need to "let go."

The worldview of those who practiced the ritual of the happy death in the eighteenth century was altogether different than this. For them, to be held in the hand of God was the cherished fate of all except those who would consciously resist, or rebel against, the divine. In this way of thinking, the challenge of dying was not relinquishing your supposed possessions but rather numbering yourself rightly among those things that belong to God. As she died, then, Mary Clulow's mother was reminding her daughter of what she understood to be life's most fundamental truth: no matter how troublesome and complicated the world might become, her life, like all of life, was in the hands of God.

When I am asked to name the single greatest difference between the typical death in our day and the deaths represented in the accounts from the eighteenth and nineteenth centuries, I reply, "the vitality and agency of the one who is dying." In part because we place such high priority on prolonging life—and therefore so quickly, almost reflexively, embrace the use of extraordinary medical technologies—the dying in our day are likely to spend their final hours, or days, or even weeks, hooked up to an assortment of disabling medical machines or in a state of subdued consciousness and muted agency. As countless studies have shown, this passive approach to dying is also cultivated by the institutional environment of the hospital, which draws so sharply the distinctions between those who give care ("caregivers") and those who receive it ("patients"). Most people in our day think of death as something that "overtakes us" or to which we "succumb."

By contrast, those who practiced the ritual of happy dying near the turn of the nineteenth century did not surrender to death; and they did not approach it in a spirit of resignation or despair. To the contrary, because they believed God's hands were strong and trustworthy, people like Mary Clulow's mother embraced death, or, better yet, they rose to greet it as if rushing into a loving embrace. As a popular hymn from the eighteenth century indelicately put it, "Get thee up and die!"

Again and again in the pages of publications like *The Arminian*, those who died happy deaths in the seventeenth and eighteenth centuries were portrayed as the principal "actors" in the dramas of their own deaths. Almost without exception, the authors of the accounts employ J. Wood's editorial strategy, excerpting their subjects' journals, striving to let them tell their stories in their own words. As their subjects approach the edge of death the authors themselves take over the narratives, but they do so in ways that preserve the dying person's central role. There is no presumption whatsoever that the physical work of bodily dying will render the dying person passive or depressed. To the contrary, in the typical account everyone present at the deathbed is portrayed as praying, singing, and conversing, but the dying person is also shown to be praising, blessing, witnessing, exhorting, and answering questions ("teaching"). The authors allow other characters to enter the story but almost always as foils, to ask questions that the one close to death can answer or to represent a kind of person who has some benefit to receive from the one who is about to die.

This narrative motif was not merely a dramatic device. Christians living in early modern England and America believed that the closer a person drew to the edge of death, the closer that person's soul was to God. As a corollary it was expected that the faithful who were nearing death should be particularly adept at representing the will of God to others. For this reason the accounts of happy deaths were primarily focused on the words and acts of the dying persons themselves.

Truly happy deaths, then—deaths deemed worthy of published accounts—were ones in which the dying could be portrayed as *leading* from the deathbed. As far as authors like J. Wood were concerned, those who died happy deaths were not just actively engaged in the communal, spiritual work of dying but indeed were responsible themselves for turning the event of dying into an experience of ritualized worship. The key acts of "ministry" at the deathbed were not those shared by others with the one who was dying. At the heart of the ritual of the happy death were the expressions of love conveyed by the dying persons themselves—what I would call "the ministry of dying."

The most obvious examples of this distinctive form of Christian ministry are cases of explicit exhortation and witnessing. But even when not engaged in such evangelizing, the people practicing the ritual of the happy death are portrayed in the accounts as ministering to those around them, and their efforts are always reported as being very "affecting." Here are a few representative examples from the 1801 issues of *The Arminian*:

> His little boy being brought to him, he laid his hand on the child's head, and said,—"God Almighty bless you, my dear boy! God bless you in time and forever!" He then gave him a kiss, and said, "I hope to see you in heaven: Farewell: God bless thee!" [May 1801]
>
> She laboured till near three o'clock next morning,

with such fervency and strength, as astonished us all. Three persons found peace with God, and several went away in distress, on account of the burden of their sins. [October 1801]

She then prayed for each individual of the family, and committed us all to God, in full confidence that the Lord would save us all. [April 1801]

Mrs. Hunter was a part of this grand tradition. Her mother's death caused her to see things very clearly: her living, her suffering, and her hopes of living beyond dying—all these were in the hands of God. Mrs. Hunter considered this fundamental truth extraordinarily good news, and she would cling to it, seven years later, as she entered her own final preparations for death. Just a few days before she died, she would tell a friend "he [Christ] supports my soul in such a manner, that it is heaven on earth to be afflicted. I have no wish to live or die: I am in God's hands; let him do what seemeth him good."

———

I never exchanged more than pleasantries with Nora Lopez. Her son, Roberto, had been worshipping at my church in Anaheim for over a year and had said on several occasions that he hoped she would have the chance to meet me. Roberto explained that his mother, who was increasingly frail, had a great respect for pastors, her husband having been a Protestant pastor in Peru for many years. She would take great delight in the fact that I spoke Spanish, Roberto said. "Some day I am going to bring her to church."

At the beginning of the new year in 2004, Roberto convinced Nora to attend worship on Sunday mornings. Walking slowly, his mother on his arm, he was visibly pleased to have her with him. On several occasions Roberto and Nora joined the greeting line that formed at the back of the sanctuary after the service. There we would chat briefly in Spanish and more than once I expressed a desire to visit at greater length. But before I had the chance to follow through, I received a call from Roberto informing me that his mother was in intensive care at the local hospital after suffering a catastrophic stroke.

That evening I stopped by the hospital to find out how Nora was doing. Introducing myself to two of Roberto's brothers, Esteban and Lazaro, I discovered that Nora had remained unconscious since the time of her stroke. She was breathing only with the help of a respirator. And so, as I stood by the hospital bedside, the two brothers introduced their mother to me.

Nora Cruz was born in a town near Lima, Peru, in 1912. She converted to Protestantism in the 1930s, when she met Rodolfo Lopez, the man who would become her husband. Rodolfo had been converted by missionaries from North America and was preparing to become a pastor himself. The decision to join Rodolfo in faith and marriage cost Nora deeply, as Protestants were a persecuted minority in Peru, like almost all Latin American nations an overwhelmingly Roman Catholic country. For her conversion to Protestantism Nora was renounced by many members of her own family and ostracized by lifelong friends. So together she and Rodolfo made their own family, having six children of their own and treating the church people they worked with as if they were next of kin. Rodolfo and Nora worked together in the ministry for almost fifty years, Rodolfo serving poor urban churches and Nora working with children in the Lima slums.

After her husband's death in 1992, Nora immigrated to the United States and joined her adult children, all but one of whom had settled in southern California. Together the children bought her a small house in Santa Ana, where Nora reestablished the open-door policy that had been the hallmark of the pastoral residences she and her husband had kept in Peru. Children, grandchildren, relatives, friends, and neighbors—all were welcome at Nora's home. "Mama always had time for everybody," Esteban said.

That night Esteban and Lazaro sat with me in the hospital room, singing their mother's praises. Though she was apparently unable to hear, I couldn't help but think how proud she must be to have raised such devoted sons. It was clear that Nora had remained the matriarch of the Lopez clan, despite the fact that she had remained in Peru for years after her children had immigrated to the United States. She was the center of gravity in the relational field that was this extended family; her impending death would be a grave shock to their system.

That night her two sons and I prayed with Nora Lopez, not knowing whether she could hear us. I prayed that Nora would place her life in God's hands, that she would be confident of God's loving embrace. And I prayed that Esteban and Lazaro would remember that at the end of the day Nora belonged to God. I did not expect her to make it through the night but promised to stop by the next morning to see how the family was doing.

The next morning I arrived at a hospital room that was standing room only. Nora had rallied unpredictably—miraculously, Roberto said—and her extended family had responded in kind. There were Nora's five adult children, several with their spouses, and at least as many grandchildren in the room.

There were also three pastors, invited by different members of the family, who were making sure they had all the denominational bases covered. Nora was sitting up in her hospital bed, still hooked up to the respirator but looking much stronger than I ever could have imagined. She was obviously in great discomfort but was entirely present and alert.

Esteban explained to me that together the family had made the decision to take Nora off the respirator, something the doctor had recommended, albeit after explaining the great risks. Nora might not be able to breathe on her own, the doctor had warned, but her chances of doing so would only diminish the longer she remained on the respirator. It was now or never if Nora was going to recover from such a major stroke.

As Esteban explained all this to me in Spanish, Nora held her hands together as if in prayer and bobbed her head up and down in affirmation. She had clearly been a part of the decision making and was entirely committed to the decided course of action.

The family had wanted some time with their mother before the doctor removed the respirator. I had arrived just as they were beginning what amounted to an impromptu service of worship. No one was quite sure whether it was destined to be a healing service or a family farewell.

Esteban acted as master of ceremonies, stepping in front of his mother's bed when he spoke, as if stepping into a pulpit. Reading from the Bible, he encouraged the members of the family to set aside any differences that may have kept them apart and invited me and the other pastors to pray. We each took our turn in the middle of the family circle, at the foot of Nora's bed. Each time the group prayed, Nora returned her hands to the position of prayer. As I led the family in singing a few verses from a familiar hymn, she waved her hands in rhythm, as if conducting a choir.

It occurred to me that Nora was really the one who "presided" over this time of family worship. Her hospital bed was the focal point, much like the altar is in a church. Esteban's words were clearly spoken on her behalf—he said what she would have said had she been able. At the end of the time together, the members of her family approached her and she tapped them on the forehead one by one, a personal benediction. Two hours later, just twenty-five minutes after the doctor removed her respirator, Nora Lopez breathed her last breath.

Looking back on it now, I see Nora Lopez through the prism of Mrs. Hunter's happy death and am reminded of another favorite song among Latin America's Protestant minority:

> *Entre tus manos, está mi vida, Señor.*
> *Entre tus manos pongo mi existir.*
> *Hay que morir para vivir.*
> *Entre tus manos yo confío mi ser.*

> My life is in your hands, Lord.
> In your hands I put my very existence.
> You have to die in order to live.
> Into your hands I trust my being.

Nora Lopez died the way she lived—by placing herself in God's hands. In her final hours she expressed great faith and confidence in God and, leading by example, she entrusted others to this same care. She was, of course, not the first person to die like this. Two centuries earlier Mary Clulow saw her mother die this way. And at the age of eighteen, she herself was already preparing to do the same.

8

AH, LOVELY APPEARANCE OF DEATH:
A DOORWAY OPENED ONTO GOD

When my dear mother was in her coffin, I went several times into
the room alone, and from my heart repeated, "Ah, lovely appearance
of death . . ."

—— FROM MRS. HUNTER'S JOURNAL

Mrs. Hunter's journal does not detail her mother's funeral, and
J. Wood's account does not include any information at all about
Mrs. Hunter's own. One thing can be said for certain about both
of them, however: they featured an open casket. This tradition
was at the very center of funeral practices in early modern England and America. As suggested by her journal entries, the open
casket figured prominently in the young Mary Clulow's recollection of her mother's funeral. Most readers today will find it
astonishing that the eighteen-year-old seems to have found the
sight of her mother's dead body pleasing in the extreme.

The verse brought to Mary Clulow's heart as she stood over

her mother's body is the first verse from "Ah, Lovely Appearance of Death," a hymn written by George Whitefield, one of the eighteenth century's most renowned preachers. Born in 1714, Whitefield was widely recognized as the greatest evangelist of the eighteenth century and was known as "the apostle of the England Empire" for his thirteen phenomenally well-attended preaching tours of the American colonies. After writing the hymn (whose full text follows) in 1760, Whitefield requested that it be sung at his own funeral, a request that was granted ten years later.

> Ah, lovely appearance of death,
> What sight upon earth is so fair?
> Not all the gay pageants that breathe
> Can with a dead body compare.
> In solemn delight I survey
> A corpse when the spirit is fled
> In love with the beautiful clay,
> And longing to lie in its stead.
>
> Its languishing pain is at rest,
> Its aching and aching are o'er;
> The quiet immovable breast
> Is pained by affliction no more.
> The heart it no longer receives
> Of trouble and torturing pain;
> It ceases to flutter and beat,
> It never shall flutter again.

Whitefield's stature ensured that the hymn became a bona fide favorite, appearing continually in journals and funeral services through the mid-nineteenth century.

That those who practiced the ritual of happy dying were fascinated with the physicality of dying—and with the human corpse—was not the result of sheer morbidity. The fascination, like other propensities, had a firm theological undergirding. For the Mrs. Hunters of the world, death was something to be anticipated—in part, as Whitefield's hymn suggests, because life itself was so filled with pain and suffering, but also because in the moment of dying the individual soul was believed to be subsumed finally and fully in the dimension of the divine. As they approached the deathbeds of their loved ones, people in Mrs. Hunter's day believed themselves to be nearing the very threshold of heaven. And as they stood at their loved ones' open caskets and gravesides, they believed themselves to be gazing as if through a doorway that had been newly opened onto God.

A few weeks into my tenure as pastor at a church near San Diego, Kimberly Wilton invited my family to dinner. Kimberly's granddaughter Kyleigh had befriended my daughter, Ellen, so the invitation seemed natural enough. But Kimberly was quick to acknowledge she had another motive for inviting me to her home: "I want you to meet my mother before she dies." After dinner the next Sunday night, she and some other members of the family took me to the back room of the house and introduced me to Edith Powell.

Edith, ninety-four years old, extremely frail and profoundly deaf, was a remarkable woman. As we stood in the bedroom's doorway, Kimberly described to me how her mother had lived her life as if it were one great adventure. For thirty years she had run her own touring company, taking hundreds of trips to all parts of the world. Not only had she led groups on sightseeing tours of Europe, but decades before they became popular she was leading down-to-earth, "grassroots" tours of Mexico and Central and South America. Her career had been launched by a most remarkable inaugural tour—between 1944 and 1946 Edith and her husband Pete, a Methodist minister, had taken their four young daughters and a family friend on an overland trip to the tip of South America and back. In a station wagon containing all the supplies they would need for the trip, they had become the first family to travel the length of the newly completed Pan-American Highway.

Kimberly showed me a picture of the family by the side of their station wagon as they waited to cross the Panama Canal. Dressed in woolen overcoats and hats (it was winter), they looked like a 1940s version of *The Swiss Family Robinson*, the overloaded station wagon approximating the Robinsons' ill-fated ship. Kimberly, who celebrated her eleventh birthday during the family's sabbatical, acknowledged that they suffered any number of mishaps along the way, but she assured me the trip had been a remarkable and life-shaping event for her and for her sisters.

Edith's physical decline had been long and slow, and now, no longer able to get out of bed, she was suffering the end of what is for many older adults a frightening descent into congestive lung and heart failure. Kimberly said her doctors could not believe she had lived as long as she had. "Everyone is ready for her to go," Kimberly said, "because we know she is ready to go."

Entering Edith's room, we found her sleeping, but—

curiously, given that she was completely deaf—she began to stir as we walked close to her bed. Kimberly's granddaughter Keley moved quickly to her great-grandmother and stroked her hand as she began to come to. I was struck by Keley's tenderness and—as I had many, many times before—I remarked on the blessing it almost always is for family members when their elders are able to die at home. In fact, the four generations of Edith's family—including Kyleigh, my daughter's nine-year-old friend—moved comfortably in and out of her room. It was clear they had done a superior job of keeping Edith a part of the family, even as she had become more and more limited across the long years of her physical decline.

Kimberly and Keley showed me a small "whiteboard" and an erasable marker, explaining that because Edith was no longer able to hear, this was the only way that they could still "talk" to her. Keley wrote something on the whiteboard, gently redirected her grandmother's gaze, and showed her what she had written. Edith, who was slowly gaining her bearings after her nap, turned and looked at me, a graying forty-three-year-old man, and then at Kimberly, her seventy-one-year-old daughter.

"Are you going to marry him?" she asked Kimberly.

Kimberly laughed and scribbled on the whiteboard, "This is the Methodist minister, Mom."

Edith read what Kimberly had written and then shouted out in protest. "Don't marry a preacher!" she yelled. "You'll be miserable your whole life!"

Kimberly, Keley, and I burst out laughing.

"I don't know why she said that," Kimberly said. "She and Dad weren't miserable—at least I don't think they were." She scribbled something else on the whiteboard and we continued the visit. I don't remember what else was written or said that night. Edith's cautionary outcry was a showstopper.

Perhaps Edith spoke more truth that day than Kimberly had wanted to admit about how difficult it was to be married to a pastor, but she exaggerated in declaring that it would make you miserable your whole life. Her own life bears witness that this is not the case. Edith was not miserable—she would not allow herself to be. Her extensive travels had turned her into a voracious lover of life and a fearless spiritual adventurer. Kimberly showed me some of the letters Edith had written to the people with whom she had traveled. The letters brimmed with happiness, as in this "farewell" letter written to her clients when she formally closed her touring business in 1977:

> It's been 30 years of fun and action and I'm loathe to let it go, but it has to be for many reasons. In those 30 years I've taken 1098 (with the repeaters it's been 1537) different persons on 140 tours . . . In those happy years I visited 76 foreign countries and had groups in 52 of them. I now have only 64 yet to conquer. Pete tells me I will need another 30 years . . .
>
> What the future holds is a mystery but the past has been all that anyone could wish for and I thank you all, love you all, and believe it or not, remember EVERY ONE of the 1098 of you personally.
>
> Most sincerely,
> Edith Powell

A few weeks after my first (and only) visit with her, I found myself standing with Edith Powell's family at her graveside. Her cremated remains were in a beautiful silver box, engraved

with angels' wings not unlike those I'd seen on Puritan tombstones from the seventeenth and eighteenth centuries. Beside
Edith's box lay Pete's, identical in every way except that the
engraved image was a cross. Pete had died five years earlier,
but the family had held on to his ashes. Today, together, they
would both be laid to rest.

After the graveside service, as we stood in the cemetery visiting, Kimberly's daughter Dalén told me that Edith and Pete
were indeed famous for their feuding. "Oh, yeah, they fought
with each other constantly," Dalén said, as I silently recalled
Edith's outburst during my visit with her. "But Grandma was
a force of nature, and nothing could keep her down." I looked
at the grave and smiled.

Edith's memorial service—held the next day at the Methodist church—was a fitting tribute to a person "nothing could
keep down." Her family had invited friends using an invitation
that Edith had penned herself many years before her death.
Reproduced and distributed with the date and place filled in,
it read:

> This invitation is worded according to Edith's request.
> *Last lefts (as opposed to last rites) will be held at La Mesa First*
> *United Methodist Church on Saturday, November 20, 2004 at*
> *10 a.m. for Edith Leighton Powell. The observance of her life is*
> *called "Last Lefts," she says, because:*
>
> > *I was left-handed*
> > *I was left politically*
> > *And I was sometimes left out.*
>
> *Cheerful clothing encouraged. Lunch will be served immedi-*
> *ately following the service.*

Just as Edith's handprint was all over the invitations to her funeral, her voice was audible in what was shared that day in church. The eulogies consisted primarily of her own words, as one by one members of the family stood and read from her letters, poems, and travelogues. One of her three daughters read, "This Is It!"—a poem Edith had begun writing in 1933 and completed sixty years later. The poem summarized the great high points of Edith's life—the times at which her spirit shouted out, "This is it!"—and asserted that "the ecstasy of achievement of a goal, a big goal, is unmatched." The poem concluded this way:

> *When I arrive at the pearly gates,*
> *Joining those who have gone ahead,*
> *I will gasp with joy and shout*
> *"THIS IS IT"*
> *And know that I am dead.*

At the close of the service another of Edith's handwritten wishes was granted:

> *I want all the people who come to stand in a circle, put their arms around each other and sing "It's Love that Makes the World Go Round."*
>
> *This is real—not a joke. Please regard it as serious.*

We did exactly as she asked.

Edith Powell lived a remarkable life—unique and distinct in countless ways—but her spiritual posture was not something she dreamed up. I did not know her well enough to trace the lineage in great detail, but I know she was the inheritor of some simple conclusions about life and death, the same conclusions that people like George Whitefield and Mary Hunter had come to centuries before: life is an adventure and new experiences, even trying ones, represent great opportunities for growth and learning; at the end of life, therefore, death can be received as something beautiful, a gift from the hand of God. Seen from this perspective, death can be both a cause for mourning and a cause for celebration. The appearance of death can be downright lovely. Because Edith had taught her family this lesson, they were prepared to celebrate her death as they were her life's other great adventures.

Several days after Edith's funeral, Kimberly stopped by at church and we talked at greater length about her mother's dying moments. Quietly, uneventfully, with her daughter Devi holding her hand, Edith had finally run out of breath. Then Kimberly had called the family, and through the rest of the day, before the mortician came, they had all stopped by to say their prayers over Edith's body. I thought to myself, "how wonderful," as I imagined this procession of personal visits, for the first time in a very long time requiring no whiteboard or markers. I imagined Kimberly and Keley and Dalén and Kyleigh and the rest of Edith's family praying over her body, and it struck me that in a peculiar way Edith's death had opened a new channel of communication to God.

Kimberly also told me her experience of calling in to church to report the news of her mother's death. The church administrator, Laura—a longtime friend of the family who knew well how long Edith had been suffering—received Kimberly's news of her mother's death and replied, "Well, good for her! And good for you! And I mean that in the best way possible!" Kimberly laughed approvingly as she told me about this conversation—Laura had captured accurately the spirit with which Edith had finished her life. Freed from what George Whitefield called the "aching and aching" of her physical body, she was now happily departed, through the open door of faith, on her last great trip.

9

A GREATER CHANGE:
IN SEARCH OF GOD'S WILL

Not long after the death of her mother, she was led to see and feel her
want of a greater change from sin to holiness.

— J. WOOD

In my work as a pastor I find that most people, when the rubber hits the road in their living and in their dying, want to know the will of God and conform themselves to it. "What should I do?" is a notorious question in the community of counselors and pastors, reflecting an almost universal assumption that there is a distinction between right and wrong. For religious people the question is accurately reframed as "What is God's will for my life?" The question is most difficult, of course, in circumstances that don't lend themselves to obvious, clear-cut decisions. Should I divorce my husband, who says he no longer loves me? Should I bail my son out of jail again? Should I support my country in this war? Should I stop these painful cancer treatments and begin preparing for death? Answers to questions like these must come from deep within the people who pose them; they force the questioners to seek integrity in their relationship with God.

I have known some people—including those whose stories I tell in this book—who faced down life's challenges with a sense of spiritual confidence that is a marvel to behold. This confidence in God does not wash away the uncertainty that comes with the human condition but rather seems simply to pick the uncertainty up and carry it downstream until it is, as Charles Wesley put it in one of his hymns, "plunged into the Godhead's deepest sea / and lost in God's immensity." These people face down death in this same way—with confident assurance, they look death in the eye and embrace it as a final gift from God.

The way J. Wood tells the story, this was what Mary Clulow had in mind when, at the age of eighteen, she decided to pursue "a greater change" in her own life. She was not yet dying, but her mother's death impressed upon her the importance of preparing to die. She determined to make a spiritual journey "from sin to holiness," and set out in search of "purity of heart." As he does so extensively throughout his account, J. Wood cites Mrs. Hunter's own words, as he found them in her journal:

> These words came into my mind,—"Without holiness, no man shall see the Lord." I was then happy, but prayed that God would make me holy. The more I prayed, the more I saw the necessity of purity of heart. I knew that God, for Christ's sake, had forgiven all my sins; yet I could not rest in that enjoyment alone.

In her living and her dying, she decided, her goal would be nothing less than a perfect spiritual union with God.

Readers of *The Arminian* were very familiar with Mrs. Hunter's aspiration. Talk of "holiness" was widespread in late-eighteenth-century England. In fact, the pursuit of holiness —also called "entire sanctification" or "Christian perfection"—was generating huge firestorms of debate and dispute. The mere idea seemed utterly blasphemous to Calvinists and others who believed that human beings, as fallen creatures, were irretrievably depraved. Methodists and others countered that holiness was the very "marrow" of scripture—after all, the words "holy" and "holiness" appear almost six hundred times in the King James Bible. And as for the controversial talk of Christian perfection, well, Christ himself, according to the gospel of Matthew, had told his disciples, "be ye therefore perfect, even as your Father which is in heaven is perfect" (Matthew 5:48). Why, the Methodists asked, would Christ command his followers to aspire to something—"be ye therefore perfect"—if in fact this was impossible to do?

At first glance this theological dispute may seem utterly irrelevant to our day, the equivalent of the notorious medieval debates over how many angels could dance on the head of a pin. But in fact this centuries-old debate over Christian perfection strikes at the core issues of faith: What is the true meaning of human existence, and what should be the goal or purpose of human life? Is it possible to rise above the powers of sin and darkness in this life, or must we wait for death to deliver us from sin's sphere of influence? Is it possible to love God and neighbor with our whole heart, as Jesus commanded his followers to do, or are we destined forever to be subject in this life to the power of our lesser selves?

It should come as no surprise that the eighteenth-century debate over the nature and possibilities of Christian perfection was never entirely resolved. Methodism's foremost champion, John Wesley, argued throughout his life that it was no greater feat for God to "perfect" a human being than it was for God to save a human being in the first place. Wesley never claimed, however, to have received the gift of "entire sanctification" himself, and he steadfastly refused to name specific examples of people who had received this crowning spiritual gift. Perhaps he thought that to do so would open him up to criticism and ridicule by those who knew the person he might name, and would, of course, be able to quickly point out their failings and limitations. Perhaps he simply did not want to fuel the fires of egotists like Thomas Maxfield and George Bell, renegade Methodist preachers who—foreshadowing some New Age philosophies of the late twentieth century—claimed to be walking the face of the earth as angels. Clearly, talk of Christian perfection can lead to spiritual hubris and excess.

I find myself following Wesley's lead—reluctant to name a name, to tell a story—now that I find it time to address the topic of Christian perfection. Did Jim Wislocki complete that "greater change from sin to holiness" before he died? Was Lucille Callen completely "pure in heart" as she showered affection on her sons in the hours before she died? Were the souls of the young boys Donny Moore and Jason Robb "perfected in love" as they died from cancer? Was the worship service that Nora Lopez presided over in her final hours "complete" in every way? Or the tea party that Nancy Martens hosted for her friends?

Of course there is a part of me that would want to answer "yes" to all these questions. If there is a greater degree of holiness than was demonstrated in the lives and deaths of these people, I have not seen it. These people have been mentors to me in ways more powerful than words can tell. They inspire in me the same feeling that Paul expressed in writing to the church at Philippi:

> I want to know Christ and the power of his resurrection, and the fellowship of his sufferings, being made conformable unto his death; If by any means I might attain unto the resurrection of the dead. (Philippians 3:10–11)

Mrs. Hunter and the people I have profiled in this book shared, too, this great, abiding desire, to be "made conformable unto Christ's death." I trust also they have "attained unto the resurrection of the dead."

But after issuing his bold declaration of intent, Paul followed immediately with a qualifier:

> Not as though I had already attained, either were already perfect: but I follow after, if that I may apprehend that for which also I am apprehended of Christ Jesus. (Philippians 3:12)

And herein lies the perplexity of the pursuit that Mrs. Hunter called "the greater change." How can people in the twenty-first century "follow after" in the life of faith? In what way might we be "apprehended" of God?

In recent generations the academic study of religion has taken
a decisive turn from the study of ideas ("doctrine") to the
study of practices. Instead of trying to figure out what religious people are *thinking*, students of religion are more and
more encouraged to examine closely what people are *actually
doing* as they pursue their faith. The *Oxford English Dictionary*
(2000) defines practice as "the habitual doing or carrying out
of something; a usual or customary action of performance;
action as opposed to profession, theory, knowledge, etc." And
more and more, students of religion are attentive to the communal or corporate nature of religious practice—as the Christian author Dorothy Bass has put it:

> Practices are those shared activities that address fun-
> damental human needs and that, woven together,
> form a way of life. Reflecting on practices . . . leads
> us to encounter the possibility of a faithful way of
> life, one that is both attuned to present-day needs
> and taught by ancient wisdom. And here is the really
> important point: this encounter can change how we
> live each day.

Of course the distinction between theory and practice cannot
be drawn too sharply. Ideas and thoughts and conceptions
influence human behavior and experience, which, in turn, give
rise to new ideas and understandings. It seems to me indis-
putable that there exists a dialectical relationship between the
two. But the nineteenth- and twentieth-century preoccupation

with doctrine, or right understanding—like the not unrelated exodus of so many young people from the churches of their upbringing—has resulted in a simple, overwhelming truth: in our day most people whose ancestors' lives were rooted in the soil of Christian tradition are themselves ill equipped to pursue the basic disciplines and practices of faith. In our day fewer and fewer people know the transformative power of prayer. Fewer and fewer know the deep spirituality cultivated in accountable discipleship groups. Fewer and fewer open themselves up regularly to the eye-opening and heart-opening experience of hands-on mission. Fewer and fewer read the Bible, expecting to hear through it a word from God. Individually and collectively, contemporary Americans—even those who attend church regularly—are cut off from the practical disciplines that were the source of such great spiritual power in earlier generations.

In preparing to die a happy death, Mrs. Hunter was not trying to resolve in her mind the idea of being "perfected in love." She was trying to resolve this matter in her heart, the place she understood to be the center of her will and intention. Day by day, she examined her heart unrelentingly, testing to see whether it was being "cleansed from all unrighteousness." What Mrs. Hunter was "actually doing" was this: she was putting into practice a spiritually disciplined way of life. This way of life gave embodied expression to the doctrine of holiness, and it culminated in an ancient ritual, the ritual of the happy death.

In the first part of this book I have tried to show that in our day some extraordinary people still die happy deaths, even as they are entirely unfamiliar with the ritual's historical roots. In

Part Two I will describe in greater detail the religious practices, or disciplines, that prepare people to die this way. A greater familiarity with these practices and disciplines can provide us with lessons on living, dying, and grieving that are as timely in our day as they were in the year 1801.

PART 2

LESSONS ON LIVING FROM
PEOPLE PREPARING TO DIE

LESSON

1

THE EXERCISE OF PRAYER:
WORKING OUT YOUR OWN SALVATION

From this time, for about a fortnight, she was much in the exercise of prayer, continuing three hours together in a morning on her knees, pleading with the Lord for the accomplishment of his precious promises.

— J. WOOD

Newly graduated in 1992 from the Claremont School of Theology—a fine, liberal Protestant seminary—I took on my first pastoral assignment at Calexico United Methodist Church, a tiny conservative congregation on the U.S.–Mexican border whose members shared a passion for the practices of prayer. I was patient with them and they were patient with me, but it was obvious to all that we didn't quite understand each other.

When I first arrived in Calexico I learned that one of my key collaborators would be a member of the congregation, Leticia Perez, who was paid a humble salary to staff the office as secretary for ten hours a week. Leticia was, like most of the congregation, of Mexican ancestry. Like most of the congregation she spoke both English and Spanish, and, like most of the congregation, her preferred language was the language of prayer.

In the beginning I would frequently ask Leticia for help with typing, or filing, or organizing this or that. And she would do this work cheerfully for a little while, then smile and apologize, explaining that she really wasn't very good at that kind of thing. *"Pero, Pastor,"* she would say, *"puedo orar por ti?"* (*But, Pastor, can I pray for you?*)

Had Leticia not been such a wonderful spirit, had she not exuded kindness and compassion with her every prayer, I would have been maddened by this frequent redirection of my energies. But because it was almost impossible to say no to Leticia, I would smile and accede to her request. In time I came to understand that while Leticia's title at the church was secretary, I would be much the wiser—and the congregation much the better—if I treated her as my associate pastor.

When, years later, I came across J. Wood's account of Mrs. Hunter's holy life and happy death, it dawned on me that Leticia Perez and Mary Clulow Hunter were kindred spirits although their lives were separated by language, culture, and the expanse of generations.

As J. Wood portrays her, Mary Clulow Hunter was unceasing in her practice of prayer. He describes her, variously, as "pleading with the Lord," "agonizing with the Lord in prayer," "going to a prayer-meeting," "praying with [others] till nearly exhausted" and "praying with divers[e] persons one after another." And in her own journal, Mrs. Hunter, as if an observer herself, comments repeatedly on her own practices of both "private prayer" and "praying with others." She describes herself, on different occasions, as being "remarkably drawn out in prayer" and "singularly drawn out in fervent prayer," as having her "whole heart engaged in prayer," and being driven "nearer to the Lord by watchfulness and prayer."

Mrs. Hunter also uses her journal itself as a medium of written prayer, frequently breaking out into direct address of God. Here are just a few examples:

- "Be thou my Keeper and my Guide, until thou hast made me fully meet to be gathered into eternal rest!"
- "O God strengthen me to do always the things that please thee."
- "O help me still to flee from the world, and live to thee alone!"

And even when she is not addressing God directly, her writing is saturated in the language of prayer. Frequently she excerpts phrases from the Church of England's Book of Common Prayer or includes in her writing phrases from familiar prayers and hymns; her journal is rife with the language of the Psalms, the great prayers and songs of the Hebrew people, as she found them in the King James Bible. Sometimes she marks these references and allusions with quotation marks—or sets them apart with indentations—but by no means is this always the case. Her freewheeling manner of journaling makes it almost impossible to draw sharp lines between the words of her own creation and words drawn from the storehouse of Christian memory.

If the content of Mrs. Hunter's prayers was bewilderingly diverse, so, too, was her manner of prayer—it seems she was capable of praying almost anytime, anywhere. Clearly she prayed within certain established frameworks—daily, weekly, and seasonal prayers as prescribed by the Book of Common Prayer; frequent journaling and correspondence; seasons of fasting and "searching" or "seeking" after God's will; and "praying the Psalms." According to her journal, though, she also prayed before, during, and after reading, and she prayed while writing in her journal. She prayed while visiting with her friends, and she prayed when her hands were "employed in domestic duties." During some seasons her prayer life was astonishingly active, as suggested, for instance, by this journal entry in the spring of 1794:

> For several months I prayed twenty times a day, besides lifting up my heart, when my hands were employed in my domestic duties. Very frequently when I went into any room in the house where I could not be seen, I dropped on my knees, and prayed for strength to hold fast the beginning of my confidence to the end, and that I might never become lukewarm.

Mrs. Hunter was a true virtuoso in the art of prayer.

One day I arrived at church for a funeral—one of the first funerals I would ever officiate—and was at my desk making last-minute preparations. Leticia walked into my office and characteristically said, sheepishly, *"Pastor, puedo orar por ti?"*

I was feeling pressured for time but had learned to accept Leticia's interruptions.

"*Claro*, Leticia," I said, and pushed my chair back from my desk. (*Of course.*)

Leticia giggled.

"*Por que te estás riendo?*" I asked. (*Why are you laughing?*)

She giggled some more.

"*Dime, dime.*" (*Tell me, tell me.*) By this time I knew how Leticia worked.

In Spanish she explained to me, "Well, I know you will think it's crazy, but I want to lay my hands on you while I pray for you, and I don't just want to lay them anywhere. I want to lay my hands on your feet."

"On my feet?"

"Yes, on your feet."

"Leticia," I said, "I have no idea what you are thinking, but if you want to lay your hands on my feet you can."

"You have to take your shoes off."

"I what?"

"Take your shoes off."

I gave in and did as I was told.

Leticia came to the foot of my chair and took off her shoes too, so that she could kneel down (she was wearing high heels). And she knelt down at my feet—all the way, so that she was sitting with her bottom on her heels and her head pressed all the way to the floor. She reached out her hands above her head and put them on my feet. And then she prayed:

> Lord, I give you thanks for sending Pastor John to
> our church. Thank you for giving him the desire to
> serve you and your people. Thank you for giving
> him the gift of preaching.

> Give him also, Lord, the gift of prayer. "How beau-
> tiful upon the mountains are the feet of the mes-
> senger who announces peace, who brings good news,
> who announces salvation."

As the years passed, and as I found myself serving churches with large numbers of older adults, I found myself often in this same predicament—sitting alone in my office, preparing for a funeral, and struggling to find words appropriate to the occasion. When all else failed, I would kick off my shoes and hark back with astonishment to that day in my office, when a humble Mexican woman knelt at my feet, quoted the prophet Isaiah, and blessed me in a way I had never been blessed before.

———

Leticia would have loved J. Wood's shorthand for Mrs. Hunter's frenzied practice of prayer—"the *exercise* of prayer." As so many people today are devoted to their regimens of physical exercise—jogging, cycling, swimming, hiking—Mary Hunter was devoted to prayer as an exercise demanding the engagement of her entire being, body and soul. And just as do today's power walkers and kickboxers, so Mrs. Hunter invariably felt refreshed after she had finished a "workout" consisting of prayer.

According to her journal, Mrs. Hunter associated the great moments of her life's journey—her "spiritual highs"—with the exercise of prayer. It was while praying over "that little book"—*Janeway's Token for Children*—that she first felt sure that she was going to heaven. It was, she wrote in her journal at the age of eighteen, with "my whole heart engaged in prayer ... [that] the Lord removed my guilt and sorrow, gave me the witness of his Spirit, and filled my soul with peace and joy." When a short while later she was "led to see and feel her want of a greater change from sin to holiness," she "prayed that God would make me holy." And this "desire of her soul" was fulfilled "in one of the seasons of retirement, while agonizing with the Lord in prayer."

Mrs. Hunter was not afraid to ask for things in prayer, but most often her "petitions" were for things she believed to be entirely in keeping with God's will—for "the accomplishment of his precious promises." For Mrs. Hunter prayer was a primary means by which she could pursue her ultimate goal, a spiritual union with God. On January 1, 1799, two years before her death, she made this journal entry:

> For ever blessed be my heavenly Father ... I am united to him, I trust by inseparable ties ... Oh that I may never forget his benefits; but may all the powers of my soul praise and magnify thee, O my God, my eternal portion. I shall dwell with thee thro' all eternity. A few more sufferings, and I shall rest in thine embrace. Glory be to God and the Lamb forever.

Her goal of resting in God's embrace came more and more clearly into view, as evidenced by this journal entry just three months later, a prayer sampling at every turn the poetry of the Psalms:

> Thou, O my God, condescendest to bless me in my going out, and coming in; in my basket, and in my store: thy blessing will go before me as a light, and follow as

my protecting angel: When I lay down it will defend
me, and I shall rest safely in the arms of my Beloved.
When trials and temptations raise a storm, thou canst
bid my soul be still; and all shall obey thee. I depend
only on thee: Thou art a sufficient and a never-failing
helper. When thou smilest, all the world may frown.
Thou art the chief object of my fear, and all my desires
are directed to thee.

Mrs. Hunter understood the purpose of her prayer to be
that of aligning herself with God, not bending God to her
purposes. As she tried to live a holy life, and prepared to die
a happy death, Mrs. Hunter lived her life to the rhythm of
prayer, saying and writing prayers of her own design that rep-
licated, for her own time and in her own tongue, the prayers
of the ancients.

———

A major challenge for the dying—and for any who are confined to bed—is that of retaining a sense of time and a sense
of rhythm to the day, the week, the month. The prayer card
I leave for people I visit in the hospital includes prayers that
help to mark the passing of each day—prayers for waking,
mealtime, and evening. Written by Arden Mead, the prayers are
simple and sweet and easy to pray.

I once visited a man named Art Koller, dying at home from
chronic lung failure. When I offered to give him one of my
prayer cards, he replied, "You already did, don't you remember?" I didn't remember but tried not to show my surprise.

Art reached to his bedside and, sure enough, pulled from

his Bible one of my prayer cards. I had given it to him, he said, almost three years earlier, when he was first hospitalized for the illness that was now about to kill him.

I was touched by the fact that Art had held on to this card, and all the more so when I saw that it was tattered and torn, the colors faded. Art had been using it daily since that visit three years earlier, a visit I had completely forgotten. He had used these prayers to anchor not just his days in the hospital, but the final years of his life.

That day—the last time I saw him alive—Art and I prayed the prayers on that card, walking our way through the morning, mealtime, and evening of his life. We came to the last prayer, the prayer for the end of the day, and prayed together:

> For all the blessings of this day, I give you thanks, O God, for bearing with me in my need, forgiving all my wrong for Jesus' sake, and showing me your constant and unfailing love. With confidence I close my eyes, trusting in your wakefulness. As once you raised up Jesus Christ, your Son, awaken me when night is past, to greet the opportunity of yet another day. In his dear name I pray. Amen.

As I prepared to leave, Art surprised me one last time.

"I'll be praying for you," he said.

I smiled and replied, "And I'll be praying for you."

Those who succeed in praying their way to death have cultivated the "exercise of prayer" long before they began to die. Art Koller had been praying all his life and so was able to seize upon the card I gave him as an instrument suited to the circumstances of his final years of failing health.

As J. Wood tells the story, Mrs. Hunter, too, turned with great attention to the exercise of prayer as she drew near to the edge of death. In December of the year 1800 she prayed "with peculiar fervor" at the lovefeast at Lambeth, this less than a month before she died. And just "a week before her departure," J. Wood reports, she "requested her friend to pray for her, that God would give her strength, and support her to the last." As Mrs. Hunter reported the incident, she made the request because "the enemy tempts me in such a manner that I seem to be bewildered." This was nothing new for Mrs. Hunter, this practice of turning to prayer as a refuge in a time of trial. Years earlier she had recorded in her journal this self-admonition: "When troubles pursue, and the enemy tempts to doubt of the favour of God, O my soul! fly to Jesus thy Mediator, who ever lives for thee to pray and cannot pray in vain."

The exercise of prayer was something that Mary Hunter had been practicing all her life. She believed that God had given her the spiritual gift of prayer—that God had "condescended to hear" her prayer and had "breathed into my heart an ardent desire, which nothing but the constant enjoyment of his favour could satisfy." Prayer for Mrs. Hunter was as necessary to the life of the spirit as breathing is to the life of the body. And as her body's breathing began to fail, she turned her attention to what she called "the sincere breathings of my soul." As she approached the end of her life she saw a prime opportunity—for her own benefit and the benefit of others—to exercise her most extraordinary gift.

———————

I commonly teach people who are dying a simple prayer called the "breath prayer." A form of focused meditation, the breath prayer consists of a single word or phrase, repeated rhythmically with each exhale of breath. The idea is to claim a good word or phrase as a gift from God and then, by repetition, to keep it at the forefront of your mind and heart. The practice of the breath prayer shares much in common with certain practices of Buddhist meditation, the good word of the breath prayer becoming a mantra—for Christians it is a mantra of faith.

I explained the breath prayer to a woman named Ida Cornelius, who was suffering greatly a few days before she died. Her mind was still clear, and she was determined to keep to a minimum her use of pain medication, but her attention was wavering as she warded off the pain. I asked her what word she thought might help her to express what was in her heart as she approached the edge of death. "Thank you," she said.

Her eyes had been closed as I was speaking to her, and I thought she had misunderstood me. I thought she was thanking me for teaching her the prayer. "Oh, you're welcome," I said, "but I was wondering what word might work for you as you prayed this prayer."

"Yes, yes," Ida said, a little impatiently, opening her eyes. " 'Thank you' is the word I want."

"Thank you?"

"Yes, 'thank you.' I want to thank God for the wonderful life he's given me."

"Oh," I said, "that makes perfect sense. Let's try it. I'll pray it with you to start."

Ida and I held hands and began to pray. As we inhaled I said, "Inhale the love of God." As we exhaled we said together, "Thank you." We repeated the prayer many times and I ceased to give the instruction to inhale. We breathed together, in rhythm, and prayed slowly, repeatedly, making the word a mantra of gratitude.

We breathed in . . . and as we exhaled we said, "Thank you."

We breathed in . . . we exhaled, "Thank you."

We breathed in . . . we exhaled, "Thank you."

Soon Ida fell asleep; she would not die for several days. But I sat a few more minutes, breathing in and breathing out, speaking the word of Ida's living and dying.

"Thank you . . . Thank you . . . Thank you."

It occurred to me that I was thanking Ida, too, for this moment of happy grace.

LESSON

2

KEEP THE WORD: MAKING THE BIBLE'S STORY YOUR OWN

One Tuesday morning, about 7 o'clock, while on my knees, these words came to my mind,—"I will; be thou clean." The enemy suggested, that they were not for me; I said to the Lord, "Surely they are for me: This is what I want, and am seeking." These words were repeatedly applied with power to my soul; and altho' the enemy strove to embarrass me with his suggestions, yet I resolved to keep them in my memory by repeating them.

—— FROM MRS. HUNTER'S JOURNAL

Most people I know—even those who would rightly be thought of as religious—are uncomfortable when public conversation turns to talk about the Bible. Some grow uncomfortable because of their prior experience with heavy-handed pastors or evangelists. But most, in my experience, are uncomfortable talking about the Bible because they think they are incapable of interpreting it. "I wouldn't know where to begin." "I find it so confusing." "I'm no expert." "I don't understand."

The Bible can indeed be an intimidating book, and modern "liberals" can make it seem all the more so, preoccupied as they so often are with mountains of historical, archaeological, and sociological "evidence." Modern "conservatives," meanwhile, seem to cling tenaciously to traditional interpretations of each and every scripture. And the radical conservatives, or "fundamentalists"—famous for the bumper sticker reading, "The Bible says it; I believe it; that settles it"—would seem to suggest that the diversity and complexity of the Bible can simply be wished away.

The account of Mrs. Hunter's happy death suggests there is another way to read the Bible, a way that simply transcends the modern debate. Mrs. Hunter's worldview was shaped pervasively by the Bible, but she was not a fundamentalist in the modern sense of the word. Modern fundamentalists read the Bible from a defensive and reactionary posture, always seeking to defend its "truth claims" against the competing claims of the modern, scientific worldview. But Mrs. Hunter was not engaged in this battle, living as she did before the forces of modern science had mounted such a successful assault on so many traditional beliefs.

Mrs. Hunter was a product of her times (as we all are products of our times), but she looked to the Bible to help her break free from the religious conventions of her day. She and her Methodist peers were the radicals of the eighteenth century, notorious for their novel biblical interpretations and routinely accused of "innovation" and "enthusiasm" in an age when both words were used as pejoratives.

So Mrs. Hunter did not cling to a litany of "Bible truths,"

as modern conservatives are inclined to do. Nor did she merely "study" the Bible, as do so many modern liberals, consulting it on an as-needed basis for factual "information" about living and dying. Mrs. Hunter entered into the world of the Bible with her heart and soul, expecting that her life would be caught up in the drama she found within its pages. It was as if she lived her life between the covers of her most cherished book.

There is no mystery as to the source of the words—"I will; be thou clean"—that came suddenly to Mrs. Hunter's mind one Tuesday morning while she was on her knees in prayer. They came from the first chapter of the gospel of Mark, as they are found in the King James Version of the Bible:

> And there came a leper to him, beseeching him, and kneeling down to him, and saying unto him, "If thou wilt, thou canst make me clean." And Jesus, moved with compassion, put forth his hand, and touched him, and saith unto him, "I will; be thou clean." And as soon as he had spoken, immediately the leprosy departed from him, and he was cleansed. (Mark 1:40–42)

Casting herself imaginatively in the role of the leper seeking to be cleansed, Mrs. Hunter embraced the healing words of Jesus as if they were spoken directly to her. This mystical experience was nothing out of the ordinary for Mrs. Hunter. Again and again in her journal, she filtered the rich complexity of her human condition through the Bible's vocabulary and stories, its rhythms and cadences.

The early-twentieth-century Bible scholar James Muilen-
berg once said: "Until you can read the story of Adam and
Eve, of Abraham and Sarah, of David and Bathsheba, as your
own story, you have not really understood it." This is how Mrs.
Hunter approached the scriptures: she did not select a set of
Bible teachings and superimpose them onto her life; she took
her life and sought to conform it to the stories she found in
the Bible. She made the Bible's stories her own.

———————

I remember a man named Timothy Toller, whose Bible was
a multimedia testimony to a complex spiritual life. When I
arrived at his home the day after his death, Timothy's wife,
Margaret, had his Bible sitting all by itself on the kitchen table
awaiting me. It was all we would need to plan his funeral.

Timothy's Bible had a family tree inside the front cover, a
feature common in many Bibles printed in the nineteenth and
early twentieth centuries, and Timothy had kept his family
history current and up to date. The Bible was packed with
newspaper clippings ranging from world events to obituaries
of friends. It also contained family photos, with notes on the
back—not just name and date and place, but little prayers of
thanksgiving: "my darling granddaughter Cheryl, a gift from
God."

The pages of Timothy's Bible were dog-eared and their margins were heavily and repeatedly marked. Some showed extreme
wear and tear; the paper on the page where the Twenty-third
Psalm was found had been smoothed to the point of transpar-
ency. As I talked to his wife about plans for Timothy's funeral,

I flipped through the pages of his Bible. I remember thinking, "I am flipping through Timothy's life."

Though we don't have Mrs. Hunter's Bible to examine, I imagine it looked somewhat like Timothy's. Certainly she was immersed in it to an extraordinary degree. J. Wood's account of her life and death makes clear that Mrs. Hunter did not so much "study" the Bible. Rather she partook of it, she savored it, and she ingested it, as if it were food and promised nourishment she could find nowhere else. She was not particularly curious about how the words got on the pages of the Bible (who wrote the Bible and why), a preoccupation of contemporary Christians and religious scholars. Her deep and abiding concern was how she herself could get on those pages, how she could make the story of her own life conform to the stories she encountered there.

Timothy reminded me profoundly of Mrs. Hunter. Like her, he understood intuitively that "words beget worlds"—that the words we choose to live by create the world of our living. Words have great power over us and within us. They constitute our very beings. To extend the metaphor of digestion: in Mrs. Hunter's way of thinking, we are not what we eat; we are what we read and hear and speak.

Mrs. Hunter and her peers at the turn of the nineteenth century were not the first Christians to interpret the Bible by viewing themselves as if they were living within it. This method of biblical interpretation reflects an understanding of scripture that has deep roots in the history of the church. Jeremy Taylor described this method in *The Rules and Exercises of Holy Living*. Under the heading "Rule for Hearing or Reading the Word of God," Taylor wrote: "Beg of God by prayer . . . that he would by his Spirit write the word in your heart, and that you would describe it in your life." A century earlier John Bunyan, the English preacher and author who wrote *Pilgrim's Progress*, one of the most published novels in the history of the English language, said famously, "I was never out of the Bible." Mrs. Hunter might have said the same.

Thomas Oden, editor of *Ancient Christian Commentary on Scripture*, remarks that for interpreters in the early church (the church fathers, as they are sometimes called), "each text is illumined by other texts and by the whole history of revelation." He compares this "patristic" method of reading and interpreting scripture to the Jewish Talmud, "a collection of rabbinic arguments, comments and discussions" about the Hebrew Bible. In this way of thinking, scripture presents to us not just the Bible texts themselves but also multiple "chains of interpretation." As these chains are passed down through the ages, each new generation engages the tradition by joining the ongoing conversation. The result is a bewilderingly (and wonderfully) "polyvalent" understanding of scripture—chains of meaning can be picked up and elaborated at any of an almost infinite number of links.

In this sense almost everything was fair game for Mrs. Hunter when it came to the Bible—her journal is marked throughout by a radically eclectic way of reading scripture. Sometimes she cites specific verses of scripture as confirming her suspicions and hunches. More commonly she employs a single word or short phrase from the Bible to conjure an image or emotion. Sometimes she quotes entire verses from the

Bible, but makes no mention of the source and refrains from using quotation marks. (This habit makes it difficult to know precisely where her own words trail off and the Bible's words come in.) Sometimes she alludes to familiar scriptures as a means of framing an event in her life.

In her journal Mrs. Hunter was constantly weaving the scriptures together, relating single texts to many others using analogy, poetics, and metaphorical reasoning. J. Wood's account reports that the words of scripture were constantly being "brought to her mind," "whispered to her in a still, small voice," or "put to her remembrance." She freely employed images and ideas from one part of the Bible as tools for interpreting other parts, and for interpreting her own experience. She was perfectly comfortable with revisionist (and often idiosyncratic and highly personalized) interpretations of even the most familiar Bible stories. She was constantly adding her own new links to the "chain of interpretation."

As freewheeling as she was in her reading of the Bible, it was inevitable that Mrs. Hunter should, from time to time, doubt her own intuitive interpretations. As she read the story of Jesus cleansing the leper, this doubt expressed itself in the form of a competing suggestion from "the enemy"—the suggestion that the words "I will; be thou clean" were not intended for her.

At first glance, it would seem the devil was right. After all, Mrs. Hunter was not looking for physical healing, as was the leper in Mark's first chapter. Neither was she looking to challenge the standard of ritual purification, the other theme of the gospel story (after healing the leper, Jesus instructs him: "go . . . show yourself to the priests . . . as a testimony to them").

But Mrs. Hunter thought of cleanliness metaphorically, as a

matter of holiness, or purity of heart. And so, when inserting herself imaginatively into the dialogue between Jesus and the leper, it was only natural for her to hear Jesus' promise—"I will; be thou clean"—as a promise to deliver exactly what she had been seeking. She continued the tale in her journal:

> I rose from my knees, and soon after opened the Bible, and cast my eyes on these words,—"Thou shalt be holy; for the Lord thy God is holy." I was filled with such a degree of tranquility, that wherever I turned, all was calm; my peace flowed as a river; Glory and thanks be to my God.

That holiness was not what the leper in the story was seeking was of no consequence to Mrs. Hunter. After all, she knew in her bones that the cleansing word of Jesus was also meant for her. So she cast the doubt from her heart and mind and embraced the words that had been given to her in her imaginative reading of scripture, pairing two commands: one from the New Testament, "be thou clean," and one from the Old, "thou shalt be holy." She liked these words—the way they fit together, the way they had been given to her—and so she resolved to keep them in her memory by repeating them.

Poring through accounts of happy dying in the year 1801, I laughed out loud when I came across J. S. Pipe's account of Edward Brocklehurst's happy death. As a young man, Pipe wrote, Brocklehurst "was remarkably hasty and passionate, addicting himself to swearing at an unusual rate."

I laughed because I recognized myself in it—on the basketball court I still swear like . . . well, like a basketball player.
It is a habit I picked up as a rebellious teenager, when the
basketball court was for me a little field of freedom. Free for
a few hours from my parents' watchful eyes and ears, I could
cuss up a storm.

Now a middle-aged man, I still like to play basketball—
when my knees and ankles allow it. And when I hobble out
onto the basketball court, it feels to me like I am walking into
the world of my youth. And my mouth knows it. Between the
lines painted on the gymnasium floor, I am addicted to swearing at an unusual rate.

People like J. S. Pipe and Mrs. Hunter were strong believers
in the power of the spoken word. As they practiced it, the art
of holy living is a matter of weaning yourself off the kinds of
words that speak ill—of yourself or of others—and instead
"addicting yourself" to words that matter, to words that give
life. Mrs. Hunter put it this way in her journal:

> I found my heart singularly drawn out in fervent prayer,
> that God would, from that very hour, entirely remove
> out of my nature every inclination to expose the faults
> of others, or to hear persons speak against anyone.

The art of holy living and happy dying is a matter of excising
from your speaking and hearing words that speak ill will, and
keeping there instead words that speak life.

From the moment I walk into a hospital room, or into
the room of someone dying at home, I can tell whether the
people in charge of the room are doing a good job of keeping the words of life. Even if I find the dying person alone, I

can tell when I am walking into a spiritual field that has been cultivated with life-giving words. There are books on the bed-side table—a Bible, a novel, a book of poetry or song. There is music playing, or a book on tape, giving the dying person opportunity to intentionally engage the gifts of memory and imagination.

By contrast some people, as they enter into the process of dying, find themselves cut off from the wellsprings of the words that have made them who they are. Family and friends conspire to alter entirely the field of words in which their loved ones live and move and have their being. These families fill the room with silence, or with the overbearing drone of the television, which is worse than silence. They act as if their ability to speak is an affront to the one who is dying, as if because the dying person cannot speak no one should. The hobbies and passions of the dying have already been buried, for there is no evidence or talk of them. It is as if these rooms have been emptied of words. These families have failed to "keep the word."

These are the most important questions for those who are preparing to die, and for those who would want to live as ones prepared to die: What are the words that have most shaped your lives, that have made you who you are? In what books or songs did you find them? Who spoke them to you? Can you hear these voices still, these voices that can speak you into being? How can you cultivate these words of life, and keep them?

———

Eventually the physical process of dying cuts us off from the words of our lives. Most commonly this happens in the hours or days before death, but some people—those stricken by Alzheimer's or other diseases causing grave mental impairment—live months and even years with diminished access to the words of life.

I think of a man named Gregory Randolph—a brilliant, articulate man and a former pastor, who slipped further and further into dementia while I was serving as the pastor at his church.

As I visited him across the course of his decline, Gregory's command of language and his capacity for understanding virtually disappeared. His wife would try to coax from him the words she longed to hear—the words of his active intelligence, the words of engaging conversation. But these words were less and less available to him.

I had a most beautiful and most crushing experience one day, when his wife asked that I come to take some books from the shelves of Gregory's personal library. Since he was no longer able to use them, she was planning to donate the books to charity. Before she gave them away, she invited me to have first pick.

I scoured the shelves and handpicked books that caught my attention—classics in philosophy, history, and biography. Most were gently worn and the margins were filled with delicate, penciled check marks. The checks marked words that were a part of Gregory, who he was and who he will always be. His wife sat with me as we browsed the books, and she cried.

As time passed, my visits with Gregory became less based on words. Sometimes our visits would consist of hardly any conversation at all. But always he would join in the Lord's Prayer when I began to pray at the close of our visit. And always he would respond in kind when his wife said, "I love you." "I love you, too," Gregory would say . . . and stretch out his lips for a kiss.

How fortunate that across the span of his life Gregory kept these words in his memory by repeating them. They did not come out of thin air to him. Like Mrs. Hunter, Gregory had cultivated a familiarity with the words that were important to him. He had repeated them often enough that they were programmed on his lips and "hard-wired" into his brain. I believe they were also hard-wired in his soul. Gregory was a learned man, but he chose to plant his life within the field of the Bible, within the field of faith. Because of this, his learning had been rooted in love. And so when the flowers of his learning withered, the love still stubbornly held to life, as a root buried deep in the soil. "The grass withers and the flower fades, because the breath of the Lord blows upon it," Isaiah says. "The grass withers and the flower fades, but the word of our God stands forever" (Isaiah 40:7).

I do not know when Gregory will speak his last words, but I know what those last words will be—"I love you," spoken to his wife; and "Our Father . . . ," spoken to his God.

Gregory's case may seem extreme, but the fact of the matter is that death eventually wins out over all of us in the battle for the words of our lips. But death need not win the battle for the words of our souls. Even when we are unable to speak, we can keep the word.

Deaths like Gregory Randolph's and Mrs. Hunter's remind us that dying is not really about silence. Dying, like living, is a matter of words. Death is a word spoken from the mouth of God, as surely as is the word of our birth. God speaks us into being, and God speaks us into dying. We can reject the word of God's grace. Or we can keep the word. How we respond to this word of God is up to us.

Mrs. Hunter died with an explosion of words. I have seen this only once, and the circumstance could not have been more different—a man named Howard, who had been tormented all his life, broke down and unleashed a flood of expletives and invective before lapsing into unconsciousness a few days before he died. His family was visibly shaken by his outburst, but when I tried to suggest that it was just dementia, they shook their heads. "He was angry his whole life," his daughter said.

The promise of a deathbed conversion still holds powerful sway in the popular imagination. People think that their loved one's dying—or their own—might well be marked by a spiritual experience altogether different from that which they have lived in their lives. In my experience, people die the way they live. There are exceptions, of course, especially among those for whom the process of dying is prolonged and who suffer great dementia before they die. But most people's dying words—the words of their final days and weeks and months—have been bred into them by years and years of practice and repetition.

Mrs. Hunter dares to ask us: What words do you want to shape your living and your dying? What words will be on your lips as you die? Will they be words of life, like "thank you" or "I love you" or "Our Father"? Or will they be words of anger and despair?

If you would have the words of your living and your dying be words of faith and hope and strength and love, Mrs. Hunter has some counsel for you: start keeping these words now. Keep them on your lips. Keep them in your heart. Keep them in your memory by repeating them. And where can you find these words, these words of holy living and happy dying? Mrs. Hunter would suggest there is no better place to start than the Bible.

LESSON

3

TAKE UP THE CROSS:
CONQUERING ALL THINGS

Thro' divine grace, in the exercise of visiting the sick and praying with them; and taking up my cross daily, I have been a conqueror, and not a captive.

—— FROM MRS. HUNTER'S JOURNAL

The day before Betty McDaniel died I visited with her in the hospital. After a terrible few days she was feeling a little better, regaining some strength and hoping to return home to be with her husband, Jerry. Even as she expressed this hope, though, she was cautious about seeming too optimistic. She shared with me her history of lymphoma, how for fifteen years she had been battling—on again and off again—the disease that was now about to end her life. She wondered out loud how much longer she would be able to beat the cancer back.

Betty had not shared this part of her story with me before. In my other encounters with her, she had shared with me the brightest sides of her life—her love of family and friends, her enthusiasm for the church and its ministries, her passion for peace and justice, and her concern for those who suffered injustice and oppression in this life. She never failed, in my many conversations with her, to express also her affection for me and my family, and to say how happy she was that we were newly arrived at her church.

In my last visit, though, Betty was more frank with me about what a long, hard struggle these last years had been, and she shared with me how absolutely miserable she had been feeling in the past few days. Something was not right in Betty's body, and she knew it. Later, in the moments after her death, her husband, Jerry, would share with me how difficult the last hours of Betty's life were. Early on the morning of the day after my visit, she had called Jerry on the telephone, asking him to come immediately to the hospital. Jerry stayed with Betty those final hours, as she fought her way to death through great pain, wanting finally nothing more than to die, that her pain might cease, that her long battle with cancer might finally come to an end.

The process of dying is often long and drawn out, and the final, physical work is often painful—though Betty's case may be extreme in both respects. In our day medication can sometimes mute the pain of dying, but this does not change what is, in fact, a simple truth—dying hurts.

People like Betty, though—whose last years of life were so vital, so happy, so full of life, even as her body suffered and died—remind us that we can be, as Mrs. Hunter put it, conquerors over the power of death, instead of captives to it. The phrasing in Mrs. Hunter's journal comes from the eighth chapter of Paul's letter to the Romans, in which he asks rhetorically, "Who shall separate us from the love of Christ? Shall tribulation, or distress, or persecution, or famine, or nakedness, or peril, or sword?" Paul then contrasts the great suffering of so many early Christians—"As it is written, 'For thy sake we are killed all the day long; we are accounted as sheep for the slaughter' "—with their triumphant spirit in the face of death: "Nay, in all these things we are more than conquerors through the power of him who loved us." Through my years of working with the dying, this has become one of my favorite passages in the entire Bible, seared into my consciousness from reading it at funeral services and gravesides.

For Paul the prospect of a painful death was nowhere near so strong as to shake his confidence in the power of God. He found this confidence supported most dramatically by the cross of Christ's crucifixion—a symbol of Roman torture that the first generations of Christians turned into a symbol of power and hope. People like Mary Hunter and Betty Mc-Daniel are heirs to this kind of spiritual confidence. As Paul concludes in the passage to his friends in Rome:

> For I am persuaded, that neither death, nor life, nor angels, nor principalities, nor powers, nor things present, nor things to come, Nor height, nor depth, nor any other creature, shall be able to separate us from the love of God, which is in Christ Jesus our Lord. (Romans 8:38–39)

As I left her in the hospital room the day before she died, Betty bid me farewell with a request—that I pray for her that night—and with a send-off. After we had prayed and as I turned to walk out the door, she shouted, "Love you!" She had bid me farewell this way before, as we parted company at church on Sunday mornings. I happen to know it was a common way for her to say, "Farewell." I'd venture a guess that these were the last words Betty spoke to a great, great many friends as she said good-bye to them on the telephone, or as she walked out to her car in the church parking lot. "Love you!"—I can still hear her voice shouting those words. "Love you!"

Betty's dying was filled with great pain and suffering, but I am not alone, I know, in witnessing to a great truth: the light of Betty's love has not gone out. Through the power of the one who loves us, Betty conquered all things. Not even death will hold her captive.

The historian Gregory Schneider has called the disciplined spiritual lives led by eighteenth-century Christians like Mrs. Hunter "the way of the cross." This way of life was characterized by "a pattern of perception, thought and feeling in which believers mortified their passions and weaned their affections away from Earth in order to attach them to Heaven." This pursuit may sound to the modern reader like a call to endless suffering and struggle. But Mrs. Hunter and her peers were convinced, Schneider says, that "momentary pain, sorrow and suffering would be transformed, by the grace of Christ, into lasting pleasure, joy and comfort." In the words of the Psalmist:

> For his anger endureth but only a moment,
> In his favor is life;
> Weeping may endure for a night,
> But joy cometh in the morning. (Psalm 30:5)

People like Mrs. Hunter practiced this way of the cross in a variety of structured settings. At home, gathered around "family altars," they read the Bible aloud and practiced the art of extemporaneous prayer, confessing their sin and experiencing grace and pardon from their loved ones. In small groups called "class meetings" they met to share their experiences in the life of faith and to hold each other accountable to the demands of a cross-shaped life. In special worship services—"lovefeasts" in late-eighteenth- and early-nineteenth-century England and, later, "camp meetings" in America—they shared personal testimonies about God's ways of working in their lives and cultivated communal experiences of spiritual ecstasy that offered little foretastes of heaven.

For Mrs. Hunter and her peers the deathbed was the last, and most important, venue for practicing the way of the cross. When the ritual of the happy death was engaged successfully, the whole gathered company worked together to play out the age-old battle of light versus darkness, faith versus despair, life versus death. The moment of dying represented the climax of this battle, and the point at which the dying person emerged victorious.

This is precisely what J. Wood and his unnamed peers were doing as their young friend, Mary Hunter, prepared for her death in the last months of the year 1800. As Jesus' disciples once followed him to the cross, they believed themselves to be walking with her to the very edge of death, into what Schneider calls "the pivotal point between heaven and hell."

Mrs. Hunter's friends expected that in the course of this journey she would know great physical pain and spiritual temptation. According to J. Wood, they were right:

A week before her departure, when [a] friend said to her,—"I hope you continue stedfast?"—she replied, "I know not: for the enemy tempts me in such a manner that I seem to be bewildered." She requested her friend to pray for her, that God would give her strength, and support her to the last. From this time she was seldom sensible for many minutes together till near her end; but it appeared from her expressions that Satan, the cruel adversary of men, laboured by suggestions and accusations to wrest from her the shield of faith, and make her passage through the valley of the shadow of death, as painful as possible.

Mrs. Hunter, though, was prepared to place these struggles in a larger spiritual context. Having rehearsed the way of the cross so determinedly in her living, she was prepared to practice it again in her dying. Like so many other Christians across the ages, she entrusted her dying days to God and looked for strength and consolation to Jesus, hanging on a cross.

Jennie Linholm suffered for years from her husband Frank's verbal and emotional abuse. Her friends had never known Frank to harm Jennie physically, and so they had never orchestrated a dramatic intervention. But all were of one mind: Frank was a cruel man and Jennie suffered greatly for her commitment to the marriage.

About two years before I arrived as the pastor at her church, Jennie was diagnosed with cancer, a cancer that would go into remission, and then recur, about three or four times in her remaining five years of life.

The way her friends tell the story, though, a terminal diagnosis had the strangest effect on Jennie—it caused her, for the first time in her life, to truly stand up to Frank. She continued to do the shopping and prepare the family meals, but apart from keeping up with basic household duties such as these, she began to live in every way as if she were not married. She established a separate bedroom, and came and went as she pleased. She left Frank to stew in his own juices when he was upset, and treated him as if he were a college roommate on the occasions he managed to be cordial. She cultivated new relationships with her two sons, traveling by herself to visit them, instead of waiting for them to come home, where they, too, suffered from their father's foul spirit. She immersed herself in the church, expanding her role in its programs and ministries even as she continued to struggle with her health.

By the time I arrived as the pastor at Jennie's church, her friends were marveling at how well she was doing. Even Frank, they remarked, seemed to be changing a little bit. He was still a curmudgeon, they all agreed, but he no longer spoke disrespectfully to Jennie in front of others, and they were aware that he had even been helping a little around the house. Once, when I asked Jennie how things were going at home, she smiled and said, "Frank is trying to be nicer, and when he succeeds I try to be nice to him." Her spirit was the same one reflected in this entry in Mrs. Hunter's journal: "When any persons strive to do me any injury, instead of feeling anger I feel pity and love toward their souls, and rejoice, when an opportunity offers, to return to them a kindness."

Jennie Linholm was learning when—and when not—to fight. For years, she had shouldered the burden of her troubled relationship with her husband Frank as if he were a heavy cross on her shoulder. For many years she had failed to stand up for herself and so enabled his mean-spiritedness and verbal abuse. But in her last years of life—faced with a life-and-death battle against cancer—she set Frank down, deciding finally that this was not the cross that God wanted her to bear. She undertook the way of the cross like "a conqueror, and not a captive," living five fruitful years before her death. She lived a life of great self-sacrifice—for the sake of her family and the ministry of her church. She learned to distinguish between the crosses that were a poor reflection of God's will for her life, and those that were rightly hers to bear.

Frank and Jennie remained married, but the love of husband and wife was never fully restored in them. At the end of Jennie's life, though, there were profound changes in their relationship. Freed up to live her own life, and fight her own fights, Jennie bore the cross of her physical dying with great grace. And Frank, no longer a burden to her, joined with her friends and family and stood quietly at her bedside as she died.

LESSON

4

SWEET REFLECTION ON THE PAST:
RECOGNIZING THE PRESENCE OF GOD

This being my birthday, I was much led out in sweet reflection on the past year. I find a growth in grace, and in the knowledge and love of God; more readiness to suffer his will, and patience in bearing when falsely accused.

— FROM MRS. HUNTER'S JOURNAL

Memory is crucial to the life of faith. The way some people practice it, remembering is mere nostalgia—regretting the present, these people make a fetish of the past. Those like Mrs. Hunter, living life as people prepared to die, practice a very distinctive type of remembering. Healing old wounds, reclaiming old gifts, these people remember the past in ways that transform the present. This is what Mrs. Hunter called "sweet reflection on the past"—as she rehearsed the story of God working in her life, she claimed anew the "knowledge and love of God."

Writing in her journal was for Mrs. Hunter the primary means by which she practiced this disciplined kind of reflection. As she wrote down her experiences, she blended the events of her recent days with memories from her more distant past and brought them into conversation with the challenges of her present life. In the journal entry excerpted at the opening of this chapter, her birthday occasioned this kind of self-reflection. In another entry she looks back on her experience of conversion: "It is now a little more than six years since I found the name of Jesus like ointment poured forth: it was truly the very balm my wounded soul stood in need of." And in this entry of August 8, 1799, she marks her wedding anniversary:

> This is my wedding day. I have been married five years. For ever praised be my heavenly Father, he has been far better to me than all my fears. My great concern, before I was married, was, lest, when I should have a young family, I should grow dead to God; but thanks be to him, he has given me to prove his grace sufficient to keep my soul alive to him in all situations. I now see it was from his love to me that he planted those fears in my heart, to drive me nearer to himself. Glory be to God, I have been going forward ever since I was married. My soul is considerably established in grace, in faith, knowledge, and love, and in a filial fear of grieving my God.

The way Mrs. Hunter thought of it, the past, as much as the present and the future, could be received as a gift from God.

In the course of getting to know the people at one of the churches where I served as pastor, I had the privilege of visiting with Bob and Elaine Lowry and their adult daughter, Elizabeth. Early in the conversation I asked Bob about his upbringing. He described a very humble upbringing in Alabama and concluded that part of his story with his early graduation from high school.

"What happened next?" I asked.

Bob proceeded to tell me about his service in the navy during World War II. Sent overseas in 1942, he had barely survived the battle of Guadalcanal, witnessing firsthand the death of three close friends. After recovering from his own wounds suffered in that battle, Bob also fought in 1944 in the Battle of the Philippine Sea. I asked him if he had received any medals, and he said, "Oh, yeah, I have a few of those." It was clear to me that he didn't want me to make a fuss by asking to see them.

Throughout this part of our conversation, Elaine and Elizabeth remained absolutely silent. As Bob spoke I became aware that they were looking at him very intently, listening with great attention, absolutely and utterly spellbound. It turned out that Bob had never before shared with Elizabeth the story of his injuries in the war, and had never told even Elaine, his wife of almost sixty years, about seeing his best friends killed in battle. He had taken these painful memories and buried them deep inside himself, where they remained until, half a century later, a stranger walked into his house and, under the mantle of pastoral confidence, asked him an innocent question—"What happened next?"

Three years later I found myself sitting at the same kitchen table, this time talking with Bob's family about his funeral. I recalled that first visit, and Bob's reminiscing about his time in the war, and asked Elaine and Elizabeth if they remembered that conversation. "Oh, yes, of course," Elaine said. "I think he really wanted to tell you all that. I think he suspected that you might be the one to do his funeral, and he wanted to get that off his chest." It was clear that the moment had been a catharsis for Elaine. As I look back on it, I recognize it as a moment of extraordinary grace for me, as well. I am still overwhelmed, as I think about it, by the trust Bob chose to place in me by sharing his story with me.

I think of Bob regularly now when I visit someone who I suspect might be thinking, "I wonder if this pastor will do my funeral." Most often these visits are routine—pleasantries are exchanged, best wishes are expressed, prayers are said. I am aware, though, that at any moment these people with whom I'm visiting might just surprise me with a deep remembrance from the very core of their lives. I try to prepare myself for the possibility of moments like these by recalling my first visit with Bob Lowry. The story of Bob's remembering is now a distinctive part of my own past, and so I try to make it a part of my present, too.

I frequently share with those who are confronting the power and reality of death an ancient prayer called the Examen of Consciousness. Associated especially with St. Ignatius, the prayer calls us to give thanks to God for the gifts of the past day, week, month, or year. The spiritual directors Marian Cowan and John C. Futrell have suggested that the prayer consists of saying to God "what we always want to say to a person we truly love . . . Thank you . . . Help me . . . I love you . . . I'm sorry . . . Be with me." I think of it as writing in a journal, but using meditation instead of pencil and paper.

I shared the Examen of Consciousness one day with Keith Nichols, who was mourning the loss of his wife, Carol. Like many widows and widowers, Keith was feeling profoundly out of sorts without his companion of over sixty years. Keith, though, identified himself as having lost something deeper than the daily rituals of mealtime and bedtime and church time that he and Carol had shared. "I'm struggling with questions of meaning," he said succinctly. "I know her life meant so much to so many, but I'm not sure what meaning my life can have anymore."

Keith rehearsed for me the last weeks of Carol's life and shared how he was now able to see in so many of her words and actions a farewell of sorts. Because she had died rather suddenly (and traumatically) in the hospital, just a day after the doctors suggested she would soon go home, Keith hadn't gotten to say farewell to his wife in the way that he had always imagined he would get to do. I asked if he thought now that Carol had in fact been getting ready to die, even though others around her were not aware this was what she was doing.

"Absolutely," Keith said. "I think that is exactly what she was doing."

I shared with Keith a scripture that came to mind, from Paul's second letter to Timothy, in which he compares life to a race:

> As for me, I am already being poured out as a libation, and the time of my departure has come. I have fought

the good fight, I have finished the race, I have kept the
faith. From now on there is reserved for me the crown of
righteousness, which the Lord, the righteous judge, will
give me on that day, and not only to me but also to all
who have longed for his appearing. (2 Timothy 4:6–8)

"So you think Carol knew she was finishing her race?" I asked.
"Yes, I do," Keith said.

"And what about you?" I asked. "Do you think you are near
the end of your race, too?"

"I don't know," Keith answered honestly. "I'll have to think
about that."

Next I walked Keith through the Examen of Consciousness,
guiding him to ask for an increased awareness of God's presence in the past month, a span of time that reached back to
ten days or so before Carol's death:

> God, my Father, I am totally dependent on you.
> Everything is a gift from you. All is gift. I give you
> thanks and praise for the gifts of this month ...
> Lord, I believe you work through and in time to
> reveal me to myself. Please give me an increased
> awareness of how you are guiding and shaping my
> life, as well as a more sensitive
> awareness of the obstacles I put in your way.
> You have been present in my life this month.
> Be near, now, as I reflect on:
> - Your presence in the events of this month ...
> - Your presence in the feelings I experienced this
>   month ...

- Your call to me . . .
- My response to you . . .

Father, I ask your loving forgiveness and healing. The
particular event of this month that
I most want healed is . . .
Filled with your love and power, I entrust myself to
your care, and strongly affirm . . .

*[Here I invited Keith to claim the gift he most desired, believing that God
desired to give him that gift.]*

"Did this exercise teach you anything about God?" I asked.

"I see that God was present with Carol," Keith said, "even
in the pain of her dying. It must be that God is with me now.
Isn't that so?"

"I believe that is so," I replied.

We took each other's hands and prayed, and then Keith
stood straight up and gave me a hug.

———

Remembering was not always a sweet experience for Mrs.
Hunter: in recalling the past she was also forced to confront her
own demons. On June 25, 1795, she made this entry in her journal—married less than a year, she was twenty-one years old:

While I have been writing, the enemy has been trying to
discourage me; but, thro' divine assistance, thanks be to
God, he put me in remembrance, that all things are possible with him. May I be enabled to hold fast whereunto
I have attained.

This passage reminded me of a time in my past—just a few years ago, in fact—when I was feeling profoundly discouraged. Overwhelmed at work, and uncertain that I should remain in the ministry, I knew I needed to talk things through with somebody—at a nearby Catholic church I found my way to a spiritual director, a nun named Sister Florence. In my very first visit I explained to Sister Florence that I was experiencing a "dark night of the soul." She asked me if I had ever known this kind of depression before. I had, and so I shared with her the following story:

"When I was sixteen my family moved for a year to Cambridge, England, where my father took a sabbatical from his work at the University of California. Some teenagers might have embraced the opportunity as a "junior year abroad," but I experienced it as emotional trauma. I didn't want to go, and I bitterly protested my parents' decision—to no avail. Torn from my home culture and from a close group of childhood friends, I spent the year rebelling against my parents' authority and determining to be as miserable as possible. As it turns out, being miserable wasn't difficult to do—I was the only American in my class at school, and I was teased mercilessly by my peers. I talked funny, wore queer clothes, played a sport (basketball) that English boys thought was for girls, and spent the year, generally, as a social outcast. The English winter was long and cold and dark, and I remember feeling that there would be no end to it."

Sister Florence asked me the same question that, years later, I would routinely ask people like Bob Lowry who came to me needing to tell their story: "What happened next?"

I replied: "What happened next was an incredible blessing. Because of my experience as an outsider, I learned to empa-

thize with those who are left out. When I came back to southern California, the world didn't look the same. I became aware,
for the first time, of those who were outcast in my school and
in my hometown. The experience of being marginalized made
me a more compassionate person, a more sensitive person, and
it put me in touch with the God who cares for the oppressed.
I discovered that God had gone with me to England, even
though I was unaware of it at the time. I am a better person
for having lived abroad that year, and I wouldn't take it back
for anything."

Then Sister Florence said something that struck me as being filled with enormous wisdom. "Perhaps someday," she said,
"you will be able to look back on this time in your life—what
seems to you now to be a dark night of the soul—and maybe,
just maybe, you will be able to say the same thing. Maybe you
will be able to see God at work in all of this and maybe you
will be able to claim it as a time you wouldn't take back for
anything."

Of course the good sister was exactly right. Shortly after my
session with her, I began to immerse myself in my work with
the dying. Because my soul was so filled with darkness—and
because I was not enjoying the other parts of my ministry—it
seemed to me entirely natural that I should choose to spend
my time with people who were looking death in the face. To
my great surprise, the more time I spent with the dying, the
more they became companions to me in my own journey
through the darkness. I went to the deathbed as a minister, but
I was the one who benefited from the encounters. My spirits
began to lift.

At about this time I also began to write down the stories of
these people I was coming to know as they faced death. Instead

of trying to conquer the darkness, I started to write my way through it. Through my writing I was "put in remembrance," as the young woman Mary Clulow had been two centuries before, of a great and abiding truth: it is always a mistake to confuse our discouragement with the absence of God. I had learned this lesson before in my life but had forgotten it until I engaged in the disciplined practice of sweet reflection on the past.

LESSON

5

ENJOY SWEET COMMUNION:
REMEMBERING THE SAINTS

*I enjoy sweet communion and fellowship with God, and it is the
earnest desire of my soul to be kept from saying, doing, or even
thinking any thing that would offend him. O my Lord, cleanse
the thoughts of my heart by the inspiration of thy Holy Spirit.
"Cleanse,—and keep me clean."*

—— FROM MRS. HUNTER'S JOURNAL

As the story of Jesus' last supper is told in the gospel of Luke,
Jesus, after the supper was over, bid farewell to his disciples:

> And he took bread, and gave thanks, and brake it, and
> gave unto them, saying, This is my body which is given
> for you: this do in remembrance of me. (Luke 22:19)

The word used in this passage—"remembrance"—is a translation of a Greek word *anamnesis*, which means much more

than "bringing to mind." *Anamnesis* implies a reconjuring of the reality that was known in a prior time. Jesus was asking his friends to do more than recall his memory—he was asking that they bring his very presence back into their gathering each time they shared the bread and the cup. So, from the very beginning of the tradition, Christians in all times and places have understood that when they share the bread and cup they are also sharing a mystical communion with Jesus and with all who have gone before them in the faith.

Mrs. Hunter and her contemporaries in the Church of England sought this mystical reunion with "all the saints" each time they celebrated the sacrament of communion. And before receiving the bread and wine, they prayed together a prayer called the "collect for purity," arguably the most familiar prayer from the Church of England's Book of Common Prayer:

> Almighty God, unto whom all hearts be open, all desires known, and from whom no secrets are hid; Cleanse the thoughts of our hearts by the inspiration of thy Holy Spirit, that we may perfectly love thee, and worthily magnify thy holy Name; through Christ our Lord. Amen.

It should come as little surprise that Mrs. Hunter excerpted this prayer so precisely in her journal. Her goal—in life and in death—was the same as the goal of the faithful who approached the table of communion: that her heart—cleansed by the holy inspiration of God—would be united with the hearts of Jesus and all who follow him. As she wrote just two days later in her journal, reflecting upon the promise of heaven: "There I shall have angels and saints for my companions, be with God my Father and Jesus my Friend, my Saviour, my all in all."

———

One day in the fall of 1999, while driving to my church on the west side of Los Angeles, I was thinking about a new arts and music ministry some people in the church had launched in hopes of benefiting children in neighborhood schools. The group was just a few thousand dollars short of reaching its goal for this first full year of the program's operation. Most of the funds that were needed were for scholarships, for children who otherwise wouldn't be able to afford the art classes being offered. Many people in the church had already generously supported this project, and I was trying to think who else I could talk to about giving to the scholarship fund.

While I was driving around—in a little bit of a daze, the way you sometimes get when you are distracted and driving streets that are very familiar—I had a brilliant thought: "I know who I should call—I should call Bill Mallon."

By the time I had arrived as the pastor at this church three years earlier, Bill Mallon had been suffering for over eight years with inoperable cancer of the spine. For six of the eight years he had been confined to his home, unable to come to church or make other trips that required him to be out of the house for more than ten or fifteen minutes. Like many long-term cancer patients, though, Bill had learned to control his pain and was a delight to visit. In my first year in Los Angeles, I visited him occasionally and heard frequent updates from my colleague—a retired pastor on the church staff as a parish visitor.

Whenever I visited with him, Bill Mallon made me laugh.

The first time I met him, after telling me how long he'd survived with the cancer, he said of his doctors, "They keep me alive and I keep them scratching their heads." On my second visit to see him, he told me a little bit about his service in World War II—he had been in the air force and had served in Europe. Then he looked me straight in the eye and said, "You're too young to have been a draft dodger, aren't you?" I said, "Yes, I am." He said, "That's good. We'll get along just fine."

Bill Mallon came to mind when I was thinking about funding the church's arts ministry because for years he had regularly written a check to support the church's children's programs. I knew he had given these funds in memory of his wife, Charlotte, whom he referred to always as "my beloved Char." Char had died several years before I arrived, so I never got to know her, but from Bill I learned that she was a passionate advocate for children and had a particular interest in seeing that children gained exposure to music. I also learned that this passion had been cultivated in her by her parents, who were missionaries in Korea and Japan, and who Bill said were "fabulous people." Bill gave regularly to the church through one of its women's groups as a way of honoring Char's lifelong commitment to children.

Well, the punch line to this story is that on that day I thought of asking him to help with funding the church's arts program, Bill Mallon had been dead for over a year. In those few moments, though, I had completely forgotten that he had died—I didn't realize my mistake until I got back to the office and even then I had to double-check my records at church to make sure I wasn't mistaken. For those few minutes, it seemed to me in a very clear and powerful way that Bill was still alive.

As I sat in my office "waking up," I began to browse through the file folder filled with my notes from my visits with Bill

and from my preparations for his funeral. I was reminded that
he died just a few days before All Saints Sunday, the day the
church remembers all those who have passed beyond the veil
of death. The prayers we said on that Sunday had included the
prayer called the "Great Thanksgiving," as it is written for All
Saints Sunday in our church's book of worship:

> *It is right, and a good and joyful thing,*
> *Always and everywhere to give thanks to you,*
> *Almighty God,*
> *Creator of heaven and earth,*
> *God of Abraham and Sarah,*
> *God of Miriam and Moses,*
> *God of Joshua and Deborah,*
> *God of Ruth and David,*
> *God of the priests and the prophets,*
> *God of Mary and Joseph,*
> *God of the apostles and martyrs,*
> *God of our mothers and our fathers,*
> *God of our children to all generations.*

I then came to this part of the liturgy:

> *Renew our communion with all your saints,*
> *Especially those we name before you in our hearts.*

As I read these words, Bill felt wonderfully present again to me.
Only this time I felt another presence, the presence of someone I had never met. I recalled that just a few weeks before he
died I had shared communion with Bill at his home—because
of his long illness, it was the first time in years he had received

the sacrament. And I was reminded that when it came time on that occasion to share our prayers of thanksgiving to God, Bill had made just one special request: "You be sure to thank God for my beloved Char, okay?"

Though I know it must seem crazy, as I sat in my office that day I lapsed back into the state of consciousness that had overcome me as I was driving around earlier that afternoon. This state of consciousness is something like the one called "automatic pilot" in the American vernacular. It requires that we be doing something so familiar—something like driving—that we don't have to pay conscious attention to the actions of our bodies. Freed from attentiveness to our physical actions, we can become inattentive and "spaced out." With practice, though, we are also able to become profoundly attentive to the stirrings of our souls and spirits in this condition. I see this phenomenon routinely in the people who come week after week to engage in the rituals of the church: they stand, they sit, they sing, they pray, they walk forward to receive communion. And when they do them well—when they do them with what a Buddhist might call "mindfulness"—these disciplines of worship become more than mere ritual, enabling those who practice them to tap into another level of consciousness, the consciousness of God.

That day in my office, I sat in the afternoon sun, looking out my window onto the church's memorial garden. I breathed deeply and considered all the people for whom the flowers had been planted, "all the saints." And for those few moments—or was it half an hour?—I swear it seemed to me that Bill and Char were sitting right there with me, very much alive.

It also seemed to me that somewhere in the distance I could hear the sounds of children singing.

LESSON

6

DRINK FROM THE CELESTIAL STREAM: SHOUTING OUT YOUR JOY

I feel my soul much alive to God. Sometimes, when I am sitting under the precious Word, I drink of the celestial Streams, which flow from the Fountain of Life. If what I now feel is but a drop from the unexhausted Ocean of eternal Bliss, O when I reach my Mansion above, my capacious soul shall drink its fill.

— FROM MRS. HUNTER'S JOURNAL

Most people today think of church—if they think of it at all—as a place to go on Sunday for spiritual nourishment. It will come as no surprise that Mrs. Hunter was far more devoted to her religion than this. But it would be a mistake to think of Mrs. Hunter as a "church lady" who spent all her time between walls lined with stained-glass windows. To the contrary, she came to think of the "celestial stream" of God's spirit as something she could tap into at any time and any place.

According to her own journal, Mrs. Hunter's spiritual journey was marked by her experiences in a variety of settings that were "extracurricular" to her formal membership in the Church of England. At the age of twelve she joined "the Methodist society at Macclesfield" (for the early Methodists a "society" was an informal gathering of people who met in ways that crossed or ignored parish lines). Later, as a young woman working as a visitor in the sick ward, she gathered a group of people together, with whom "she met once a week as a class"—classes were the Methodist equivalent of today's "support groups," in which people gathered for mutual sharing and accountability. On the last Sunday of 1800, just a few weeks before her death, she shared her testimony at "a lovefeast at Lambeth"; lovefeasts for the early Methodists (and "camp meetings" for later generations) were outdoor gatherings for singing, preaching, praying, and socializing.

Her experience in each of these venues served to confirm and strengthen Mrs. Hunter in her pursuit of holiness. In these places—set apart from her daily routine—she could act out the truth of her self-understanding as a child of God. Here, among friends, she could tap into ecstatic experiences of the Holy Spirit and rehearse the kind of enthusiastic expression that would come to mark her dying days. Affording her experiences sharply distinct from those that would have been available to her otherwise, these settings represented for Mrs. Hunter and her peers, in the apt phrase of R. Garretson, one of Mrs. Hunter's American contemporaries, "a little heaven below." Anticipating that after death, in heaven, her spirit would be completely satisfied, she was determined in the here and now to "drink of the celestial streams, which flow from the Fountain of Life."

Beatrice Schuyler was positively ebullient as I visited with her one afternoon in October. Newly arrived as the pastor at her church, I had been told that Beatrice's doctors were about to abandon curative treatment of her ovarian cancer. I went to get to know her, anticipating that I might in a few months be presiding at her funeral. I was especially looking forward to the visit because the previous Sunday Beatrice had come to the communion rail for prayer after receiving the sacrament during morning worship. When I had seen her at the rail with her hands outstretched (asking for prayer), I had expected to find her despondent in the face of her cancer's ever-worsening prognosis. Instead she had asked that I offer "prayers of praise and thanksgiving because God is being so good to me through all of this." This request for prayer led me to believe that Beatrice might be another person who could teach me something about the nature of the happy death.

Beatrice welcomed me into her humble apartment with great enthusiasm. She had been looking forward to my visit, she said, and had a great deal she wanted to share. "It's been a long time since a pastor came to my home," she said. "I can't believe you're here!"

Beatrice quickly outlined for me the story of her life, openly sharing her history of struggles with depression and anxiety. But she said the last four years had been the best years of her life. She had gone on a new medication at that time, but she attributed her spiritual renewal to much, much more. "It's not just the medication—it's my family, my church, and the medication, and it's not any one of those things, but it's all of these things working together, and it's God working through all these things for my happiness. Thank you, God," she shouted out. "Thank you, God, for working through these things!"

Beatrice was animated in a way that, quite honestly, took me aback. As she reviewed her life—past and present—she found delight and wonder at every turn. She shared with me the story of her family, her older brother and sister and her younger sister. "They have been through so much with me and yet they still love me. Sometimes I can't believe it, but they do . . . and I guess it makes sense, because I love them, too."

She was preparing for an appointment with her oncologist the next day, prepared for whatever might come. "I'm going with Lois [a friend from church], and she's promised to celebrate with me if it's good news, and to cheer me up if it's not." She had met with a surgeon the week before who had told her, "There is no point in operating on your hernia—you won't be around long enough to worry about that." Even this she laughed off, saying, "How's that for bedside manner!"

Anticipating Lois's visit, she recalled a visit from another church friend, Miriam, who had visited her the last time she was in the hospital. A shy woman, Miriam prayed reluctantly at the end of their time together, and only after Beatrice had specifically requested that she do. "She prayed quietly," Beatrice said, "but beautifully. That was one of the best visits I ever had."

She had several books on her coffee table that she was anxious to share with me. Several were related to her current condition—*Scarred by Struggle, Transformed by Hope*, by Joan Chittister, and Richard J. Foster's collection, *Devotional Classics*—but she was reading several others simply because she found them remarkable and wonderful. We compared notes about Jared

Diamond's *Guns, Germs, and Steel*, discovering that we shared a passion for history. About another book—*The Spirit Catches You and You Fall Down* by Anne Fadiman—she said, "I don't know if I'll ever get to this, but it looks so wonderful I'm looking forward to giving it away."

I asked about her parents, and Beatrice recalled her mother's death. She had had ovarian cancer too but died of a brain hemorrhage before the cancer killed her. She had gone to the hospital in Redlands, where she had died peacefully, "very contentedly"—she had a good death and Beatrice very much remembered that.

I asked about her relationship with the church, and she reviewed her experiences with different pastors. "I always learn something from pastors," she said. "A lot of people at our church had problems with Dan Simpson, but I remember some of his sermons and I remember having an awakening, a heartwarming like John Wesley or Augustine had, while he was here. I remember him sharing his personal experience of being alone at camp and walking out at night under the stars and feeling the presence of God, who reassured him, 'even if no one else likes you, I do!' I remember feeling alone too at that time, and his telling that story made a real difference in my life."

As we talked, Beatrice grew more and more animated. Every time I introduced a new topic of conversation, Beatrice would gasp with delight and launch into a story from her life. She asked several times if she was speaking too loudly, saying her ears were clogged from a cold and she couldn't tell if she was shouting. She was, but I didn't mind, and reassured her that she was doing just fine.

Beatrice kept shouting. "I'm sorry, I fear I'm talking too

loud. I need to pop my ears!" But she was so excited she just couldn't stop. She was so excited that I had come to visit. I was flattered and delighted and astonished and pleased.

In what she believed to be the final months of her life Beatrice was doing what Mrs. Hunter called "drinking from the celestial stream." She had been given a new set of glasses, and through them she saw things clearly. Her life was rich and varied and filled to overflowing with good things. "God works through all of these things," Beatrice said. "I wasn't always aware of that, but I am now, and I know that God is in all of these things."

And as we named these things—a litany of ordinary, everyday things through which Beatrice saw God at work—she just kept on shouting, ending every story by crying out, "Thank you, God! Thank you!"

She just kept shouting.

Beatrice Schuyler's ecstatic outbursts were not the product of mental illness, nor were they "delusional"—they reflect a mode of expression entirely in character for some people who have cultivated practices of enthusiastic prayer and praise. As had Mary Hunter two centuries earlier, Beatrice had, throughout her life, rehearsed this way of being and so she readily adopted the same spiritual posture as she prepared to die.

As we now know, Mary Hunter was far from alone in this practice of spiritually "rising" to greet death. Quite to the contrary, she was part of an emerging religious movement, Methodism, whose adherents in the second half of the eighteenth century became notorious in both England and America for their ecstatic spiritual experiences—and specifically for their happy deaths. In America these practices of spiritual exuberance became especially controversial because, in their determined cultivation of them, the Methodists embraced the mixing of European and African modes of worship.

In recent decades religious scholars have taken a fresh look at early American religious history. Because this history was, for generations, written by the historical "winners"—the descendants of America's early Puritans and Calvinists—the role of other players in the story has been persistently overshadowed. More recent scholarship has unearthed the stories of these unheralded historical actors, digging back through primary documents—diaries, letters, church records, and the like—to tell the history of American religious experience "from the bottom up."

At first glance the religious experience of a young Englishwoman in London in the late eighteenth century may seem to have been, necessarily, miles apart from that of her African contemporaries living under American slavery. Though she would have read about the religious experience of American Methodists in *The Arminian* magazine, it is safe to assume that Mrs. Hunter was largely unfamiliar with the African-influenced traditions of "shouting" and "getting happy." Still, one would be mistaken to believe there is no connection between these religious practices and Mrs. Hunter's practice of the happy death. Consider, for instance, that she compared her own spiritual struggle to that of the Israelites, as described in the Bible story of the Exodus:

June 23. This morning my mind was much refreshed in reading of the children of Israel, when Pharaoh with all

his host pursued them; they cried to the Lord and were
delivered . . . When my consolations are at a low ebb, and
my way is cloudy, if the powers of darkness pursue me,
as the Egyptians did the children of Israel; fear not, O
my soul, but stand still, and see the salvation of God.
He will again visit me, and shine with double luster, and
my peace will flow like a river.

The Exodus is widely recognized as the "governing narrative" of the African-American church—as the Israelites were
freed from bondage in Pharaoh's Egypt, so black slaves sought
freedom from slavery in America; as the Israelites searched for
a promised land "flowing with milk and honey," so African-
Americans continue to search for an America in which someday "justice will flow down like waters, and righteousness like
a mighty stream."

These words will be most familiar to Americans, perhaps,
because they were deployed rhetorically by Martin Luther
King Jr. in his famous speeches during black America's struggle
for civil rights. Fewer will have recognized that King himself,
under the constant threat of death and in the last years of his
life preparing (rightly, it turned out) to be martyred for the
cause, was also tapping into another deep tradition, the tradition of the happy death. Consider this conclusion to a sermon
he preached on the eve of his assassination, at Mason Temple
in Memphis, Tennessee:

Like anybody, I would like to live a long life—longevity
has its place. But I'm not concerned about that now. I
just want to do God's will. And He's allowed me to go
up to the mountain. And I've looked over, and I've seen

the promised land. I may not get there with you. But I
want you to know tonight, that we, as a people, will get
to the promised land. So I'm happy tonight; I'm not
worried about anything; I'm not fearing any man. Mine
eyes have seen the glory of the coming of the Lord.

Certainly it is safe to assume that Mrs. Hunter was largely unfamiliar with the culture of Africans and African-Americans.
She understood something of their spiritual struggle, though.
In her living she desired nothing more than to visit the spiritual mountaintop—and so, too, in her dying.

Lorene Julia Ryan was born in 1905 in rural McClusky, North
Dakota. Raised with twelve siblings on a family farm, she
learned there—in the estimation of her oldest daughter, who
ninety-eight years later would write her obituary—to "depend
on God for her very sustenance."

Lorene was married twice. The first marriage was unusual
for her generation, in that it ended in divorce. The second,
which would last, was even more unusual—in 1942 she married Wallace Martin, a black man and a Methodist preacher.
For over three decades Lorene faithfully tended to the needs
of the congregations where her husband served as pastor. Active in the choir, the United Methodist Women, and the Wes-
leyan Service Guild, she served the traditional role of pastor's
wife—one of the few white women to do so in predominantly
African-American churches.

By the time I arrived as the pastor at her daughter's church
on the west side of Los Angeles, Lorene was ninety years old,

profoundly hard of hearing, and very nearly blind. She was also among my favorite parishioners because she had retained the habit, cultivated in the black church, of verbally "exhorting" the preacher. For my four years in Los Angeles, Lorene sat in the front pew on Sundays—the "amen corner"—egging me on and encouraging me to push well beyond my culturally conditioned comfort zone in extemporaneous preaching and prayer. If Lorene was altogether quiet on Sunday morning, I knew I hadn't really opened myself up to the moving of the Spirit. If she was whispering, I knew I was on to something, and I kept moving in that direction. If Lorene was shouting "Amen!" or "Hallelujah!" I knew I had gotten it right.

When I learned of Lorene's death in September 2004, I called her daughter, Carol, to inquire about her mother's funeral.

"It was a wonderful funeral," Carol said, "very much in the old school. Reverend Simms preached a good old-fashioned sermon and that's what mother would have wanted. She always said she was a 'shouting Methodist.' "

"That's how I remember her from my time at the church," I said.

"She shouted a lot when you were there," Carol said.

I have never, ever received higher praise.

Conventional conceptions of death and dying, based largely on the work of Elisabeth Kübler-Ross, hold that people will need to pass through a varied sequence of stages when confronted with the inevitability of death. If these stages can be worked through, it is thought, the dying person will achieve a posture of "acceptance" and will "become neither depressed nor angry, neither happy nor sad, but void of feelings—'all felt out.' "

The Kübler-Ross consensus, though, presumes as a point of departure the fear and denial of death—"abhorrence and avoidance," even. This may be the spiritual point of departure for a majority of Americans, but it is by no means universal.

Lorene Martin and other spiritual descendants of Mrs. Hunter propose an altogether different way of approaching life and death. In their way of thinking about things, the goal of living and the goal of dying are the same—to know the happiness of spirit that comes from drawing close to God. This kind of spiritual fulfillment is something to be sought after daily, through the disciplined practice of a religious way of life. For those who practice this way of life and see it through to its logical conclusion, death is not something to be passively accepted, but rather something that can be triumphantly transcended.

Formed spiritually in the black church, Lorene's life was marked by her search for ecstatic experiences of the Holy Spirit, what Mrs. Hunter called "drinking from the celestial stream." Across the generations African-American Christians have learned to tap into this stream of heightened consciousness as a means of bearing the unbearable and rising above circumstances of suffering and oppression. Lorene Martin was a disciplined practitioner of this spiritual way of life, and so she tapped the celestial stream to rise above the suffering of her death. The night before she died, Carol reported, she told her family she was "resting in the arms of Jesus." For Lorene Martin, this was not a fate to be "accepted," nor did it result in feeling "all felt out." In her living and in her dying, Lorene was happy—happy to find herself in Jesus' embrace.

LESSON

7

THE LABOR OF LOVE:
LOVING GOD AND NEIGHBOR

Her leisure time was partly employed in visiting the Sick-Ward in one of the Workhouses, where she regularly attended once or twice a week, talking to the poor women and praying with them, till nearly exhausted. Her labour of love in this way was crowned with the divine blessing.

— J. WOOD

At every church where I have worked as a pastor, and in every religious community with which I am familiar, there is a dedicated group of people—most, but not all, of them women—who spend hours and hours each week visiting the sick, the lonely, and the elderly "shut in" to their homes. This work is routine and mundane, and, when viewed from without, it seems entirely unremarkable. But viewed "from within"—from the perspective, that is, of those who give and receive these visits—this work offers glimpses of the very essence of the religious life, creating windows onto the very face of God.

As J. Wood emphasizes again and again in his account of her life and death, Mrs. Hunter was a dedicated practitioner of this ritual of visitation. He presents her work as largely selfless and self-sacrificing, but also desires to make clear that she learned a great deal from her encounters with the sick and the dying. Through the work of visitation, he suggests, she herself was transformed and inspired and came to understand more and more clearly the nature of true happiness, that is, contentment with God. In the following story, one of the few that he tells without reference to Mrs. Hunter's journal, J. Wood recounts the events of one day in April 1799:

> As Mrs. Hunter was going to a prayer-meeting, at Queen-Street, she saw a young woman who was apparently in great want. Mrs. H. advised her to go into the workhouse; the poor creature said, she had an aged mother to support, and was come out that morning to beg something for her. As such accounts in London are numerous, and most of them fallacious, her story was not believed; but Mrs. H. felt uneasy in her mind, and thought, if it should be true, it was a pity the aged woman should die of want. She, therefore, after meeting, went in search of the poor woman, and after much fruitless enquiry, at length found her and her poor daughter in a garret: the mother was eighty-two years of age, happy in God, and waiting for her blessed change from the pains and sorrows of mortality, to the unmixed joys of the heavenly society.

This encounter, obviously significant for Mrs. Hunter, was of paramount importance for J. Wood. Here, in stark relief, was a crucial lesson about the nature of true happiness. Irrespective of one's physical condition, true happiness was to be found in God. And it was no coincidence, to his mind, that Mary Hunter found this truth most magnificently illustrated in the midst of doing good.

A colleague once asked me to substitute for him as the preacher at a monthly worship service in the "healthcare center" at a nearby convalescent home. Every month for many years he had led this worship service, together with a small group of women from our church. There they sang hymns with the oldest and most infirm residents, a congregation whose membership changed almost monthly due to the "graduations" of death.

When I began my work as a pastor I feared these kinds of invitations, uncertain what I should say to those suffering great debilitation as they neared the end of life. As the years have passed, though, I have learned to receive these invitations with joy and gladness. I know that when I am asked to preach at a convalescent home, I will be preaching to an open and receptive congregation, even if many are unable to demonstrably express their enthusiasm and appreciation.

The day before the visit, my colleague emphasized that most of the people I'd be preaching to would be suffering from various kinds and degrees of dementia. "Their attention spans won't be very long," he said, "and they seem to appreciate it if I repeat myself a lot. If I were you I'd pick a favorite verse and just really drive it home." This reminder gave rise, I do believe, to one of the best five-minute sermons I ever preached, informed as it was by my reading of Mrs. Hunter's journal and her sense that as she approached the end of life she was preparing to enjoy a true spiritual communion with God.

Had I been preaching a more complicated sermon I would have included this quotation from Thomas Merton, who, in an essay on St. John of the Cross, writes:

> At the heart of the Christian faith is the conviction that, when death is accepted in the spirit of faith, and when one's whole life is oriented to self-giving so that at its end one gladly and freely surrenders it back into the hands of God the Creator and Redeemer, then death is transformed into a fulfillment. One conquers death by love—not by one's own heroic virtuousness, but by sharing in the love with which Christ accepted death on the Cross.

Instead, this is what I preached that day, as I faced a room full of people in wheelchairs, one of them crying softly for no apparent reason, many slumped over and apparently sleeping, and most paying what can be described, at best, as intermittent attention:

> Once upon a time someone asked Jesus what was the greatest commandment in the law. Do you know what he said? He said, "You shall love the Lord your God with all your heart and all your mind and all your strength." This is the greatest commandment in the law. And a second is like it: "You shall love your neighbor as yourself."

Love the Lord your God. Love your neighbor. Jesus said there is nothing more important than these two things. Love God. Love your neighbor. It just doesn't get any better than that.

I know that you are in a time of life that often seems difficult. Some of you are lonely, I know. Some of you are in pain. Some of you are frightened about what tomorrow might hold for you, what is next in store for you in this life or the next.

I think it's important for you to remember what Jesus said was the most important thing in this life—to love the Lord your God with all your heart and all your might and all your strength . . . and to love your neighbor as yourself.

I know there are many, many things that you cannot do at this time in your life. Maybe you can't walk anymore. Maybe you can't take yourself to the bathroom, or get in and out of bed without asking someone for help. Maybe you can't do the work you always used to do. Maybe you can't talk the way you once could, even just to tell your friends and family that you love them.

But you know what? For all these things you can't do, you can still do the most important thing of all. You can love the Lord your God with all your heart, and you can love your neighbor as yourself. No disease can take this ability away from you. And you don't need anyone's assistance to do it, either. If I may be so bold as to give you just one piece of advice this morning, this is what I'd like to say: at this time in your life you can still concentrate all your energies on the one thing that really matters: to love the Lord your God with all your heart and love your neighbor as yourself.

I've been reading the journal of a woman who died a long, long time ago. She spent the last years of her life visiting people who were sick, just like we are here visiting with you today. You know what she told a friend a few weeks before she died? She said, "I cannot account for it, but I had an impression on my mind . . . that I had something to do, which I have now done; and it seems that I have now nothing more to do on earth."

Of course I don't know whether or not you are at this point in your life. Only God knows the hour of our dying. But I'm guessing that some of you may feel you have done what you had to do, and that you now have nothing more to do on earth. If you are at this point, or think you might be, I want to ask you to remember one thing. It is the most important thing you have ever done, and you can still do it. You can do it right now. You can love the Lord your God with all your heart. And you can love your neighbor as yourself.

I looked around the room, and I could not tell if my message had struck home with the residents of the healthcare center. Their expressions had not noticeably changed. There was no applause, there were no "amens," though I think I saw a nodding head or two.

My sermon had struck a nerve, though, with Joyce and Laura and Phyllis and Ruth, the women from my church who were assisting in the worship service. Mostly older women, they had been greatly affected by my sermon, some for very personal reasons with which I was quite familiar. Phyllis was well into her eighties and had come close to dying herself just the year before. Ruth, who played the piano that day, was growing forgetful and was aware that this was the first sign of Alzheimer's, a disease that ran in her family line.

Right through the challenges of their own aging—right in the face of their own dying—these women had been coming to this convalescent home for years. They knew the people in the wheelchairs by name, helped them find the right page in their songbooks when it came time to sing hymns, prayed with them in their loneliness, and held their hands in their dying. They were the ones who were incarnating the message I preached that day, the ones preaching not with words, but with flesh and bone.

I looked around at these women—Mrs. Hunter might have been among them—and I could tell that they were genuinely moved. I thought, "Now there are some people who know what is most important in this life."

And I gave thanks to God for the labor of love.

LESSON

8

LIVE THE PRESENT MOMENT: SEIZING THE DAY

August 2. I have learned to live the present moment by faith, and am saved by grace. O create in me more sincere gratitude and love to thee, my heavenly Father.

—— FROM MRS. HUNTER'S JOURNAL

Mrs. Hunter's language rarely sounds fresh and current—most often I found myself needing to "translate," or at least interpret, her eighteenth-century turns of phrase. But in her journal entry of August 2, 1800, she used an expression that has survived two centuries intact. We tend to think of "living in the moment" as a contemporary approach to spirituality, warning us against dwelling too heavily on the past or worrying too much about the future. In fact, the idea of seizing each moment, and each day, is an age-old spiritual practice, and Mrs. Hunter considered it central to both holy living and happy dying.

For Mrs. Hunter, of course, to "live the present moment by faith" was something of a necessity. J. Wood gives no indication that she suffered what we would today call a "terminal illness." Rather, as she passed through her adolescence and entered early adulthood, it was simply and abundantly clear to her that she was unlikely to live a long life. In her day few people did. Given the incidence of mortality in eighteenth-century England, it made perfect sense for her to cast her life in the light of death.

For this reason more than any other, the Mrs. Hunter of J. Wood's account—a woman in her early twenties—reminds me profoundly of some of the oldest people I have known in my work as a pastor. Like them, she did not expect to live much longer—and like some of them, she had somehow, mysteriously, reached a point in her spiritual journey where she would have considered this kind of expectation a burden. As far as she was concerned, a preoccupation with longevity was, like so many other temptations, a distraction from the primary purpose of living—right relationship with God. So, too, the concern with physical well-being was clearly subordinate for her to the well-being of her soul.

Of course I would not wish for a return to Mrs. Hunter's day, a day in which illness routinely cuts short the lives of otherwise healthy youth and young adults. Still, I find myself admiring Mrs. Hunter's spirit, just as I have always admired the faith I sometimes find in my most aged parishioners. People who understand themselves to be dying are often deeply appreciative of life's simplest pleasures. "If only everyone living," I find myself thinking after visiting people like these, "would seize the gift of a single day."

In setting the stage for the story of Mrs. Hunter's death, J. Wood excerpts her journal entries from the year 1800, doing so in a way designed specifically to show that she was making progress in her spiritual growth. Here is a sampling of journal entries from her final six months of life:

> *June 21.* This morning . . . my heavenly Father gave me to see what I have long wished to know, the way how I might glorify him . . . I immediately kneeled down to thank him and entreat that if I was wrong, he would direct me. It came sweetly to my mind, "This is the way: walk thou in it."

> *[June]* 29. O for more heavenly wisdom and spiritual understanding, to discern between what is only temptation, and what is sin!

> *Aug. 2.* I have learned to live the present moment by faith, and am saved by grace.

> *Sept. 3.* After private prayer, as I was coming down stairs in sweet tranquility of mind, the still small voice gently whispered, "Thou art my love, my fair one; there is no spot in thee!" Returning again to my room, almost immediately after I kneeled down, it was brought to my mind, "Thou art made whole: watch and pray lest thou again fall into temptation." My Lord and my God!

Oct. 4. Although poorly in body, I enjoy health of soul: though in the world, yet, through divine grace, I am not of the world. Glory be to my God, the sincere breathing of my heart is, that my body may be a temple for the Holy Spirit to dwell in, while I am absent from the regions above. When Jesus shall take me to himself, I shall behold his glory, and dwell for ever with him.

[Oct.] 31. My soul lives in the happy enjoyment of God. Jesus is mine, and I am his. I love him, and he loves me:—

> *O may we never parted be,*
> *'Till I become one spirit with thee.*

Dec. 4. Glory be to God, I see more and more into my ignorance, weakness, and helplessness; but the Lord is my teacher: He is my strength, my all in all. O that I may ever see myself in his own light, and feel a momentary dependence on him!

Dec. 21. I see and feel the necessity of that atonement Jesus hath made for me.

> *This all my hope, and all my plea,*
> *Jesus hath liv'd, hath died for me.*

My soul rejoices in Christ, and has no confidence in the flesh.

Lest the reader miss his point, Wood concludes this sequence with the following commentary:

It was remarked by several of Mrs. Hunter's most intimate friends, for some time before her illness, that
her growth in grace was considerable, that she was visibly ripening for the heavenly garner: a much greater
deadness to the world, and more heavenly-mindedness,
appeared in her on all occasions when she was in their
company.

As far as J. Wood was concerned, Mrs. Hunter had discovered
the secret of faith. Each moment of life was a gift from God,
to be received with wonder and gratitude. So, too, could be the
moment of her death.

One day my colleague Ed Davis took me to meet Velma and
Walt Jansen, longtime members of my new church in La Mesa,
California. Walt greeted us at the door and welcomed us in,
explaining that Velma was in the bedroom getting ready for our
visit with the assistance of her caregiver. Walt looked me over
through dark-rimmed glasses with thick lenses, then smiled at
me and shook my hand with a very strong grip. His hands were
large for a man of his height and build, and his palms hard
and calloused—from years and years of fishing, I would soon
discover. As I followed him down the hall, I thought to myself,
"Now there's a spry old man." I guessed he must be eighty,
maybe eighty-two, and was impressed that he was so physically
vital at that age.

Walt Jansen, though, was not eighty, nor was he eighty-two,
nor even eighty-five. He was ninety-three. I had never seen

anything like it. In my work I had seen a lot of people in their eighties and nineties, and a good number over one hundred, but I had never seen a man so physically vital at such an advanced age. Velma was ninety-two and they had been married for sixty-eight years.

The specific reason for our visit was that just two weeks before Walt had suffered what appeared to be a stroke, while out fishing on the ocean with his son. His whole left side was suddenly paralyzed, and his speech was dramatically slurred. His son rushed him in to shore, and an ambulance took him to the emergency room. At the hospital, though, when Walt was hooked up to an IV drip, he regained his strength suddenly and completely. One moment he was unable to move his left side and virtually unable to speak. The next moment he was pointing at the IV drip with his left hand and telling the nurse with great precision, "You know, I think I'd like another one of those." The doctor concluded he had had a blood clot in the brain, and that once the clot was dissolved his otherwise excellent circulation system just kicked right back into gear.

Like many men of his generation, Walt loved to tell jokes and kept us laughing through the visit. Much of his humor revolved around his age, and the presumed proximity of his death.

"Every morning," he said, "I get up and look in the newspaper for my obituary." I had heard others use this wisecrack, but Walt continued with a story the likes of which I had never encountered:

> You may think I'm joking, but I'm not. See, one day
> my obituary did appear in the newspaper. Of course
> it wasn't mine, but it was of a man named Walt Jansen,

and it happened that he was a Methodist, so when word got around that Walt Jansen the Methodist had died, everyone assumed it must have been me. That Sunday at church they announced that I had died, and Katherine Winslow, one of Velma's dear friends, came by after church to pay Velma a visit and express condolences on behalf of the church. Well, she rang the bell and of course I went over and opened the door. You should have seen the look on her face. She was so flustered I thought she'd faint. We had to bring her in and sit her down on the sofa and get her a glass of cold water. I think it took her weeks to recover. So that's why I get up every morning and check the newspaper for my obituary.

Ed and I laughed long and hard.

Walt went on to explain that he was looking forward to going duck hunting the next weekend, and that he was going over Velma's objections. He said that ten years ago he had visited a friend in a convalescent home and seeing people lined up in the halls in their wheelchairs made him decide that he was going to push himself and stay as physically active as he possibly could. "I'd rather die fishing or hunting than spend years and years in one of those places," he said. "Besides, once I reached eighty-eight I decided I was on borrowed time, so I treat every day as if it might be the last one I've got."

LESSON

9

BEAR TESTIMONY:
SHARING A GOOD WORD

The last Sunday in the year 1800, Mrs. H. attended a Lovefeast at Lambeth, where she bore her testimony to the goodness and power of God in cleansing from all unrighteousness, and keeping those who cleave to him in perfect peace, and stedfast hope of unclouded glory.

— J. WOOD

Just a few weeks before her death, when she sensed that her time was short, Mary Hunter was called on to speak at a love-feast in Lambeth—a church meal approximating the ritual of communion. As was traditional at such gatherings, the meal included a time for "testimony," in which individuals attempted to put into words their experiences of how God was working in their lives. That a young woman about to die should be included in this ritual was nothing out of the ordinary. In Mrs. Hunter's day those who were near the edge of death held places of great esteem in their families and churches and communities. Believed to be in a position of spiritual privilege, the dying were considered uniquely qualified to share with others the mysteries of faith and so were often called on to speak in public.

The physician Robert K. Pretzlaff has observed that the gains in longevity afforded by modern technologies like the breathing machine are often achieved at "a cost not yet fully explored: the absence of the dying person's last words." The cost is even greater, though, than Pretzlaff's observation suggests—in our day we commonly confine and medicate the dying for days or weeks or even months before their deaths. While in the hands of sensitive practitioners this treatment can often make pain manageable, it can also—and in fact often does—radically limit the ability of the dying person to communicate effectively. "Palliative care" is becoming ever more sophisticated and nuanced, but still its practitioners face daily decisions that often boil down to a simple choice: do we limit pain or consciousness? Sometimes—when the choice is always and everywhere to limit pain—what is lost is not just "final words," but the chance for the dying to witness their own final days or weeks of life.

The way Mrs. Hunter and her peers thought about it, it was not just a dying person's last words that were considered valuable but indeed the whole testimony they could offer in the course of their dying. So it was that the people who gathered at Lambeth on the last Sunday in December 1800 would have presumed that Mary Hunter—physically ever more dependent on others—was spiritually well equipped to witness to the love of God. As J. Wood tells the story, they were correct in this presumption: "At the request of the person who kept the Love-fest, [Mrs. Hunter] prayed with peculiar fervor: the influence of the Holy Spirit was eminently on the congregation, which made it a time of refreshing from the presence of the Lord."

———

About a month after I visited with her in her home, the members of Beatrice Schuyler's "circle"—named after Ethel Hawks, one of its legendary former members, now deceased—gathered at church one day after worship. Having informed Beatrice that they wanted to meet to honor her, they had placed an open invitation in the church newsletter:

> *A Celebration of Strength Honoring Beatrice Schuyler*
> *Beatrice's cheerful spirit in facing cancer*
> *has given us all a gift of strength.*
> *November 7, 2004—Fellowship Hall—12:15 p.m.*
> *Salad Potluck—rolls, desserts and drinks will be furnished*
> *All are welcome*
> *Sponsored by the Ethel Hawks Circle*

The potluck meal would be a rough approximation of what Mrs. Hunter and her peers would have called a lovefeast.

Before and after the meal, Beatrice stood near the door, visiting—it struck me she was playing a role like the one I usually see family members play at the receptions after funerals, as people stop by to "pay their respects." Beatrice, though, was hosting her own farewell—and an excellent host she was.

Near the door, Beatrice had prepared a table with photographs from across her life and had brought some of her favorite books and works of art. One of her friends asked her about two pieces that Beatrice had set upright on the table—one a colored print of calligraphy and the other a photograph of two aged hands.

"These are touchstones for me," Beatrice said. "They've been with me forever, it seems."

Pointing to the first piece, she said, "This one came first, I think. This is by Sister Corita Kent, I'm not sure if you are familiar with her. She did a lot of posterlike things, where it's all writing but varied colors and things like that, swatches, kind of modern art—serigraphs, they're called." The brightly colored serigraph displayed an excerpt from the script of Paddy Chayefsky's 1961 play *Gideon*, highlighting in large, bold print the two key lines. In the scene an angel of God queries Gideon, the play's ambivalent main character:

THE ANGEL: O! Gideon, would you have your God a
             wandering magician, slapping a timbrel and
             kicking his heels?
GIDEON: Do not rise in wrath against me, sir.
THE ANGEL: I am not in wrath. I am plainly confused. And
             sore at heart.

I HAVE LOVED YOU

             and you have turned your back.
GIDEON: I do find you personable, sir.
THE ANGEL: Personable! Gideon, one does not merely fancy
             God. I demand a splendid love from you,
             abandoned adoration, a torrent, a storm of love.
GIDEON: (with almost unbearable kindness) I'm afraid
             I'm not the splendid sort, my Lord. You want

a less moderate man than I. I'm sure you shall
find one soon enough, for you are an attractive
God, and there are many men who will love you
vigorously, I'm sure of that.
(He offers his hand and smiles disarmingly.)
Come. If I have given you some hurt, then clasp
my hand and say it is over with.
(The Angel cannot help but be amused by this
ingenious fellow. He clasps Gideon's arm.)

THE ANGEL:

I SHALL MAKE YOU LOVE ME

"Anyway," Beatrice continued, "Sister Corita was a Catholic
nun, and this one comes from the start of Paddy Chayefsky's
Gideon. And I think that's the way it works—'I have loved
you . . . I shall make you love me.' That's called 'process theology,'" Beatrice explained, referring to the philosophy of Alfred
North Whitehead, whose work asserts that God exercises influence through persuasive love—acting to "lure" people into
lives of faith—rather than exercising aggressive "power over"
human subjects. "God's love is not coercive," she went on. "I
think it's more like always being *surrounded* by love. That's what
happened with me, anyhow.

"And this one," Beatrice said, pointing to the photograph
of weathered hands, "reminds me of my parents, because all
through their lives they were a mixture of brainpower and just
hard work. My father was a rancher for many years. My mother
washed clothes in an old hand-crank washing machine, kept a
kitchen garden, the whole bit. So I look at that and I see tired,

worn hands, but I also see praying hands, and that's what carries me through."

After the people had served themselves lunch, members of Beatrice's circle made a few presentations. Then, just when the formal proceedings were about to close, one of Beatrice's friends, well into her eighties, came to the podium using a walker and asked for assistance in placing a piece of paper on the podium. On it she had written these words, which she read aloud:

> Dear Beatrice, I've written several editions of this note to you, wanting to say thank you for touching my life in so many ways. You've helped me wrap Christmas packages, not once but many times. Do you remember? We went to eat health food together several times, after we visited the art gallery. We spent that time laughing together, and I don't even remember what we were laughing about, but I remember laughing with you. I do remember you bought a T-shirt, something special. Do you still have it? I have loved your cheery voice, both here at church and on the phone—sometimes I called you and sometimes you called me, which was nice.

At this point she asked for help in turning over the paper on the podium and then continued: "You have enriched my soul, dear friend. I send my blessings. I love you as you travel through this life. With love and admiration. My name is Edna Phillips." Edna looked up across the room and smiled, and then she said, "And I want to come rub your head." The crowd laughed. Edna made her way to where Beatrice was sitting and said, "Is it all right?" Beatrice said, "Yes, it is." So Edna rubbed Beatrice's head—hair shortened to stubble by chemotherapy. Then she leaned over and gave Beatrice a kiss.

As J. Wood tells the story, Mrs. Hunter did not, as we would say today, "succumb" to death. Rather, she embraced it:

> About nine days after [the lovefeast at Lambeth] she was taken ill of a putrid fever, which very soon brought on a delirium, accompanied with great depression of spirit; yet she had some intervals of recollection, and in all those seasons was happy in God. In one of these a friend asked her if Christ was precious? To whom she answered,—"Yes, very precious: he supports my soul in such a manner, that it is heaven on earth to be afflicted. I have no wish to live or die: I am in God's hands; let him do what seemeth him good."

The contemporary literature would describe this spiritual posture of Mrs. Hunter's as one of "acceptance." Filled with talk of "stages," this literature assumes that the dying will have to confront significant emotional issues (such as grief and loss and forgiveness) as a part of their spiritual preparation for death. And indeed, in our day many people diagnosed with terminal illness have to make this kind of spiritual journey in short order, having never been encouraged to confront and accept the inevitability of their physical deaths.

But Mrs. Hunter was not like most people in our day: by the time it became clear she was dying, she had already completed—through years of practiced spiritual discipline—the emotional and spiritual work necessary to prepare herself for a happy death. According to J. Wood, Mrs. Hunter was entirely unfazed by what she saw coming:

> It seems probable, that she had some presentiment of her approaching dissolution, for just before she was taken ill, she said to an intimate friend, "I cannot account for it, but I had an impression on my mind, when at Bedfordbury prayer-meeting, that I had something to do, which I have now done; and it seems that I have now nothing more to do on earth."

Her physical health failing at the turn of the year 1801, Mrs. Hunter considered that she was being liberated—liberated to turn her attention to others, and liberated to bear witness, in word and deed, to the love of God.

Physicians and others who work with the dying continue to debate the extent to which people are able to exercise control over their physical death. Every pastor, rabbi, and physician I know, though, has stories to tell about people who seem to have orchestrated the timing of their demise. I think of Eleanor Bragg, who died the day after her sixty-fifth wedding anniversary. As I met with Eleanor's family to plan her funeral, it became clear to me that just as Eleanor had been hanging on physically to celebrate her anniversary, so her husband, Cleve, had been hanging on to see Eleanor through to death. Within a few months he, too, was dead.

My colleague Ed Davis once shared with me the most

memorable death in his fifty-five years of ministry—the story of Jennie Seitz, who died on Christmas Eve. As we sat and ate hamburgers and french fries at a local bar, Ed described to me how his wife, Gloria, had befriended Jennie while they were living in Hemet, California. Jennie had owned and operated a dress shop next door to the travel agency where Gloria had worked. Over time, through her friendship with Gloria, Jennie became a member of Ed's church.

Jennie Seitz was diagnosed with cancer late one summer and within months had come dangerously close to death. In talking with Ed about her hopes and wishes for the end of life, she made clear that she had set a marker for herself—Christmas Eve. She explained that in her family's tradition, the children and grandchildren gathered at her house to exchange gifts on Christmas Eve. As the oldest member in the family, it was her job to distribute the gifts. She told Ed she was determined to see this tradition through.

Knowing that Jennie's hold on life was very fragile, Ed decided to visit her between services on Christmas Eve. There he found Jennie, surrounded by two generations of family, resolved to fulfill her ambition. Sitting up in a chair, she read the names on the gifts, and as her children and grandchildren came forward one by one to receive them, she said to each, "Merry Christmas." After presiding over her favorite family ritual, Jennie went to bed. An hour later she was dead.

I asked Ed if the family knew how close to dying Jennie had been.

"They knew she was critically ill," he said, "but I'm not sure they knew her death was as close as that."

"They knew it was coming, though?" I asked.

"Oh, yes. That was clear. They knew she had had her sights

set on that evening, and they knew it was her last Christmas. It was evident as they came forward to get their gifts."

"But she knew what was happening, didn't she?" I asked.

Ed nodded. Jennie knew she had had something to do, which she had now done.

It was her turn to receive a gift.

LESSON

10

FEAR NOT: CLAIMING THE VICTORY OVER DEATH

Fear not, for I am with thee. Behold, I go to prepare a place for thee, that where I am, thou mayest be also.

—— MARY CLULOW HUNTER TO A FRIEND A FEW DAYS
BEFORE HER DEATH, AS RECOUNTED BY J. WOOD

Mary Hunter did not fear death; rather she thought of it as she thought of life itself, as something delivered from the hand of God. Conversing further with her friends—almost assuredly members of her Methodist "class"—Mrs. Hunter blended Bible verses. The phrase "fear not" appears over one hundred times in the King James Version of the Bible—it is spoken by Moses as the Israelites approach the Red Sea (Exodus 20:20); it is a salutation commonly shared by angels, as when the angel came to Mary, the mother of Jesus, assuring her that her most unexpected pregnancy was the work of God (Luke 1:30); it is a phrase spoken more than once by Jesus, as in this word of comfort to his disciples: "Fear not, little flock; for it is your Father's good pleasure to give you the kingdom" (Luke 12:32).

The remainder of Mrs. Hunter's words come from Jesus' farewell address to his disciples, as found in the gospel of John:

> Let not your heart be troubled: ye believe in God, believe also in me. In my Father's house are many mansions: if it were not so, I would have told you. I go to prepare a place for you. And if I go and prepare a place for you, I will come again, and receive you unto myself; that where I am, there ye may be also. (John 14:1–3)

Mrs. Hunter spoke these verses without referencing their scriptural contexts, without mentioning that the words were the words of Jesus. She spoke them as if they were her own words, because she had made them her own. "Fear not," she said to her friends. "I go to prepare a place for thee, that where I am thou mayest be also."

It was time for her to take her leave.

Mabel Craft, a legendary figure in the life of Anaheim United Methodist Church, died in February 2001. This is the brief obituary that was printed on the back of the bulletin distributed at Mabel's funeral:

> Mabel Ella Short was born on January 5, 1921 in Indianapolis, Indiana. In 1948 she moved to Southern

California with her husband, Nick Craft, and two sons, Louis and Dave. A few years later the family moved into a house on East Wilhelmina Street in Anaheim to live with Mabel's mother, father and mother-in-law. Mabel would live in this house for the rest of her life.

Mabel described herself as a worker, saying, "I've worked all my life." Professionally, Mabel worked as an administrator in, among other places, a hosiery company and a tamale factory. In 1991, at the age of 71, she retired from her position in the Anaheim office of Ling Electronics.

Mabel was also a legendary worker at church. The house on Wilhelmina Street was right around the corner from the Wesley Methodist Church. Mabel remembered hosting every kind of church activity imaginable: "Santa got dressed in my living room and we cooked Thanksgiving turkeys in my kitchen." When, in the early 1970s, Anaheim's Methodist churches merged, Mabel quickly became a pillar in the new church community of Anaheim United Methodist Church. She was devoted to Bible Study and worship, was active in the Anaheim United Methodist Women (including a three year stint as president) and was a principal player in the church's annual holiday bazaar, where her jams and relishes were always among the first items sold.

Mabel worked hard at home, too, raising her two sons and her grandson, Robert. She took great joy, in later years, in once again sharing the house on Wilhelmina Street with her son, Dave, and was especially pleased when she succeeded in converting him into a Los Angeles Lakers fan.

Mabel underwent major surgery in 1998 and claimed the last years of her life as gifts from God, calling them "the best years of my life." When her cancer recurred late in 1999, she came quickly to the decision to forgo aggressive chemotherapy and let the cancer run its course.

She died as gracefully as she lived, in the house on Wilhelmina Street, on February 1, 2001.

Sometimes what goes around comes around. God loved Mabel and Mabel loved God back. Mabel loved people, and people loved her back. Mabel Craft was a beautiful, practical, funny, warm, loving person, and a constant in the life of this church. She will be greatly missed.

On the one hand this brief obituary is like no other, because it describes a particular individual. As is every person, Mabel Craft was unique—and uniquely precious in the eyes of God. On the other hand, Mabel's obituary is like thousands and thousands of others that are printed every year in funeral bulletins and church newsletters across the English-speaking world. These obituaries conform to a predictable formula—they recount basic biographical facts and in broad strokes paint a picture of the deceased's life; they extol the deceased's virtues and successes, while conveniently omitting vices and failures and character flaws. Copied and distributed far and wide, these obituaries serve a whole host of purposes. They console family and friends, reminding them of the long sweep of their loved one's life and death. They provide for those less familiar with the deceased—extended family, friends from the past—a brief description of the person's death. They spare pastors (and others) the work of repeating a life story in the funeral's formal eulogy.

These obituaries, though, serve another, more fundamental, purpose—the same purpose as did accounts like J. Wood's account of Mrs. Hunter's happy death: they serve to remind whoever may come across them that God is the author of the beginning of life, and God is the author of the end. To live and die in the hands of God is not to be a puppet, subject to the whims of a fickle puppeteer. To live in God's hands is to make oneself amenable to the purposes of a loving God—it is like being a pencil, or a pen (or a keyboard, I suppose), an instrument willing to be used for the creation of something that witnesses to eternal truths. At the root of the ritual of happy dying lies the understanding that those who are dying are just as capable as the physically healthy of serving as instruments of God's will. In fact, Mrs. Hunter and her descendants would suggest that in some ways the dying are uniquely qualified to serve these divine purposes.

Almost two years after Mabel's funeral, I gathered with a group of women at my church to discuss the book I was writing about the ritual of the happy death. After I described some of the historical background, the conversation quickly turned to people they had known who had died this way—"happy" in God. Mabel topped the list. She was, they all agreed, completely undaunted by the prospect of dying.

"Mabel was a very practical person," said Lou-Anne, the church's parish nurse. "She had a very practical approach to life and a very practical approach to death. She just went about her business. She kept making her jams and jellies. She continued going to the theater. Right up to the end she was giving people rides to church—that's why she kept that big old car all those years."

"She spent her last days giving away her favorite plants," remembered Wilma. "I got some irises and rhubarb."

Lucille butted in: "That rhubarb wasn't hers, you know. She got that from Phyllis Brown before Phyllis died. I don't know where Phyllis got it, but that plant has been going around for years."

Everybody laughed.

"Fearless," said Lorraine. "Mabel was absolutely fearless in the face of death."

"That's the way her parents were, too," said Ilene. "I remember back to when they were dying. They were all living in the same house and Mabel was the one who cared for them. They died exactly the same way she did, you know. Mabel was just following suit."

Mabel was just following suit. I liked the way Ilene had put it, and as I looked around the circle it was not hard for me to imagine that some of these women, too, were following suit in the life of faith. They were almost all in their eighties and were having to think quite concretely—quite "practically"—about preparing to die. I remember wondering which of these women would follow the lead of their good friend Mabel Craft.

Six months later—during which time I had taken a new position as the pastor of another church—I received a phone call from Lou-Anne, who thought I would want to know that Barbara Ferry had died. Barbara was a member of Mabel Craft's circle, but she hadn't been at church that day we talked about happy dying—by that time she was already diagnosed with terminal cancer and had been moved by her family to a convalescent hospital in a nearby town.

"Oh, John," Lou-Anne said, "I wish you could have seen her. She was another one. She was so happy those last few weeks. Her spirits were soaring. And she had such hopes for her funeral. She really wanted it to be a witness to her faith. I really think she was doing what you are writing about in your book."

"I remember thinking exactly that," I said, "the last few times I visited with her. I remember her telling me how she had decided not to have any chemotherapy because she didn't want to go through all that. And I remember her telling me that in the midst of her dying, her two estranged sons had reconciled—there was some long-standing disagreement between them, I can't remember what. When she told me that, I had just been reading an account from the eighteenth century where that was one of a dying woman's main hopes—that two of her family members would be reconciled."

"Barbara was a great lady," Lou-Anne said. "I saw her just a few days before she died, and she was so happy. She just wasn't afraid to go."

The ritual of happy dying has survived across the generations because people like Mabel Craft and Barbara Ferry have been "following suit" in the life of faith. Without a conscious intent to instruct, the dying have presented themselves as living examples of a way of life that culminates in deaths that give glory to God, "happy deaths." Without being formally "taught," the living have been inspired to pursue this same way of life and death, rooting their lives more deeply in the love of God and neighbor.

This process by which the rituals of faith are transmitted is not easily documented, and so it is easily misunderstood, if not altogether overlooked. The process is similar to the way a sturdy plant can be passed around from family to family, friend to friend, generation to generation.

My work has convinced me that this process of transmission is particularly powerful in giving shape to the rituals of death. At the end of life, people commonly turn for guidance to their role models in faith. Barbara Ferry looked to Mabel Craft, just as Mabel had looked to her parents, just as Mary Hunter remembered her mother's deathbed blessing, just as Christians across the ages have looked to the earliest generations of disciples, so many of whom were martyred for the faith. Christians, of course, trace this chain of influence to Jesus, whose death has caused millions to ponder the true meaning of life. As J. Wood reports Mrs. Hunter to have said in conversing with friends about her imminent death: "What a precious Saviour is Christ to my soul! Away with all beside; away with it. What could I do now, if I had not this Saviour?" Wood continues:

> When asked if she thought her sickness would be unto death, she answered—"I know not: I have not an anxious thought about it; I only desire that God may support me through life and death."

When I started my work as a pastor, I went to visit the dying feeling very much alone. Now, when I am called to the bedside of someone who is "actively dying" (to use the modern medical vernacular), I think of Lucille Callen and Jason Robb and Jim Wislocki and Nancy Martens and Mabel Craft. I think of J. Wood and Mrs. Hunter and her mother, and I think of the Venerable Bede and the early Christian martyrs. I think of Jesus and I say with Mrs. Hunter, "Away with all beside; away with it!" And then—whether we are surrounded by a large and loving family, or whether the dying person and I are the only ones in the room—I open my Bible to these words from the fifteenth chapter of Paul's first letter to the Corinthians:

> Listen, I will tell you a mystery! We will not all die, but we will all be changed, for this perishable body must put on imperishability, and this mortal body must put on immortality.
>
> Then the saying that is written will be fulfilled: "Where, O death, is your victory? Where, O death, is your sting?"
>
> But thanks be to God, who gives us the victory over death through our Lord Jesus Christ.

THE PROSPECT OF GREAT USEFULNESS

Thus died Mrs. Hunter, in the prime of life, (about 26 years of age)
and in the prospect of great usefulness. Her soul was bent on doing
good, and her leisure time was employed in visiting the sick and needy.
Mr. Hunter assured me, that during the years he was married to her,
he had never seen a temper, nor heard a word from her, inconsistent
with the Christian Character. May God raise up many more such
examples of pure and undefiled religion.

LONDON, MAY 4, 1801

J. WOOD

A conspiracy is afoot to break the silence in which the modern world has cloaked the topic of death. The spread of the hospice movement is the most striking sign of this conspiracy's success, but there are plenty of others: the popularity of writings by Elisabeth Kübler-Ross and her protégés; the inclusion of courses on care for the dying in nursing and medical school curricula; the increasing assertiveness of family members and religious professionals in hospitals and other settings of institutionalized care. Cases like that of Terri Schiavo—the Florida woman who died in March 2005 after thirteen years in what doctors call a "persistent vegetative state"—send shivers of recognition across the modern world, causing millions to complete "advance directives," legal documents specifying those medical instruments—breathing machines and feeding tubes, most notably—to which they do not wish to be subjected. More and more, people find themselves talking about death— at home, at work, in churches, synagogues, and mosques—even if they struggle to find the words with which to do so. What is death, we ask one another, that we have allowed ourselves to become so pathologically fearful of it? And why, for so many generations, did we stop talking about it?

By reclaiming the tradition of the happy death, we can break the modern silence about death, and we can break it with songs of praise and thanksgiving. In the face of death we can sing with the ancients that God is the beginning and the end of our lives, the very source of our being and our eternal home.

It was no whim that led J. Wood to write up the story of Mrs. Hunter's life and death. From his perspective—a perspective he shared with the editors of *The Arminian* and with many other Christians across the history of the church—a happy death was not a marginal or inconsequential expression of faith. The way J. Wood thought about it, deaths like Mrs. Hunter's were reflective of an entire way of life—one he believed to be

entirely "consistent with Christian Character," and one representing "pure and undefiled religion." In writing an account of
the life and death of this one young woman, he was hoping to
inspire others to follow in her footsteps.

My purpose in writing this book has not been altogether
different from this. I am convinced that the practices leading
to a happy death can make a real difference in our lives today—because I have caught glimpses of this difference in the
lives and deaths of the people I have profiled in this book. Before learning about the ritual of the happy death, when I witnessed someone like Jim Wislocki or Nancy Martens die with
such extraordinary spiritual uplift, I would think to myself,
What a shame more people can't die like that. As I immersed myself in
the accounts of happy dying from the turn of the nineteenth
century, I became convinced that more people can.

Of course another unavoidable thought presents itself when
reading J. Wood's account of Mrs. Hunter's happy death: *What
a shame she had to die so young.* And this thought presents a great
dilemma.

For generations modern medicine has been dedicated to
the cause of prolonging life—almost single-mindedly so. This
dedication has reaped a great harvest: the fight against disease
and death has prolonged by decades the average life span in
Europe and North America, and it holds out the promise of
doing so again in the coming century. In recent generations,
however, this commitment to longevity has been brought more
and more into dialogue with concerns commonly referred to
under the rubric "quality of life."

Even in my fourteen years as a parish pastor, I have de-
tected a sea change in the culture, with more and more people

making decisions that shorten their own lives, or the lives of their loved ones, for the sake of improving the quality of the last months or years of life. Decisions (like Mabel Craft's and Barbara Ferry's) to forgo aggressive chemotherapy—with all the accompanying side effects—and to let terminal cancers run their course are only the most obvious instances in which concerns for the quality of life are more and more often given priority over the desire for longevity.

The practices of the happy death introduce yet another variable, though, into this already complex equation—a variable I would call "quality of death."

Surely in some circumstances neither concerns for longevity nor concerns for quality of life are the critical factors in end-of-life decisions. Surely in some circumstances the crucial question is not "how long can I live?" nor even "what quality of life can I enjoy in the time remaining?" but instead, quite specifically, "how well can I die?"

This question is by no means inconsequential. As I have tried to show in this book, the rituals of death are rooted in a host of disciplined practices that define an entire way of life. While not referring specifically to the ritual of happy dying, the poet and essayist Wendell Berry has drawn this same connection:

> The question of how you want to die is somewhat fantastical but nonetheless it is one that all the living need to consider . . . Do you want to die at home with your people "in blessed peace around you". . . . Or do you want to die in the hands of the best medical professionals wherever they are? Such questions seem irrelevant until you realize that they define two very different lives.

Berry's observation, drawn from his book *Life Is a Miracle*, strikes at the heart of the matter: the kinds of lives we lead help give shape to the deaths we die, and the kinds of deaths we seek help define the ways we live.

In the spring of 2005, as I was finishing work on this book, these issues were brought to the forefront of public attention when, just two days after Terri Schiavo died, so too did Pope John Paul II. Where Schiavo's death provoked great public controversy, the pope's manner of death met with near universal admiration. Dying as he did with great grace and dignity, John Paul II gave people the world over a glimpse—albeit filtered through the lens of the mass media—of a "happy death." In the pope's dying days, he greeted the crowds in St. Peter's Square from his window in the Vatican and received the sacrament of communion. He also made careful decisions about the kind of medical care he desired to receive, and that which he did not, living out the words he had written in 1999, in a letter addressed to the world's elderly:

> It is wonderful to be able to give oneself to the very end for the sake of the kingdom of God. At the same time, I find great peace in thinking of the time when the Lord will call me: from life to life. And so I often find myself saying, with no trace of melancholy, a prayer recited by priests after the celebration of the Eucharist: *In hora mortis meae voca me, et iube me venire ad te* (at the hour of my death, call me and bid me come to you). This is the prayer of Christian hope.

Mrs. Hunter would have applauded Karol Wojtyla, the man who died as Pope John Paul II. For her the true goal in life was altogether different from a long life, and it was altogether different from what modern people commonly think of when referring to "quality of life." More than anything else, Mrs. Hunter wanted to know a spiritual communion with God—to be "perfected" in the love of God and neighbor. Once having experienced this communion, she felt she was prepared to die—as she said in her journal: "I had an impression . . . that I had something to do, which I have now done; and it seems that I have now nothing more to do on earth." To the modern ear this sounds fatalistic, even nihilistic, but in Mrs. Hunter's worldview the sentiment expressed is one of spiritual transcendence.

Across the centuries, this tradition—the tradition of the happy death—has been practiced by faithful people in an enormous range of cultural circumstances and has been given a broad range of theological expression. The practice of this tradition does not do away with the tensions that exist between the competing concerns that so often present themselves at the end of life—as J. Wood acknowledged, for instance, Mrs. Hunter died "in the prospect of great usefulness," and in this one can hear a wish that she might have lived a longer life.

But happy deaths can be extraordinarily useful in their own right—for this reason J. Wood chose to write up the story of Mrs. Hunter's life and death. That ordinary people, not just popes, can be "useful" in their dying—useful to God and helpful to others—is a thought that almost never enters modern conversations about the end of life.

So I believe that J. Wood's phrase—"the prospect of great usefulness"—can be meaningfully applied to the tradition of happy dying itself. It is time we reclaim this historic exercise of faith. To do so will require, of course, that we confront anew our own mortality, and the mortality of those we love. Even more, though, it requires that we ask questions like these:

- What can I learn from my loved ones who have died, or are nearing death?
- What will be *my* spiritual posture as I prepare to die?
- What will I say and do in my dying months? my dying days? my dying hours?
- What will my death look like and feel like to those who love me?
- What effect will my dying have on others?
- What will be my dying words?
- Will my dying be pleasing in God's eyes?

Whatever they might be, our answers to these questions will necessarily give rise to another question, one with endlessly far-reaching implications:

- What, then, can I start doing now—what words can I begin to rehearse; what ways of life can I begin to practice?—that will prepare me to die this kind of death?

For her part, Mrs. Hunter answered this question decisively, and experienced what she believed to be the logical consequences. As she put it in her journal, in an entry dated April 29, 1800:

I offer myself and all I do, to God. My soul longs for a fuller union with God; more faith and love! O the delight, the happiness I feel!

EPILOGUE

MEETING MRS. HUNTER AGAIN

On New Year's Day 2005, I flew to England with my father—our stated purpose: to find Mrs. Hunter's grave. It seemed the only fitting way to bring to a close my years-long obsession with a twenty-six-year-old woman who had been dead for over two hundred years.

In preparing for the trip it occurred to me how little hard information I had to work with. I knew she had been born Mary Clulow on June 21, 1774, in Macclesfield, a town thirty miles south of Manchester. I knew she had married on August 8, 1794, to become Mrs. Hunter. I knew from J. Wood's conclusion that she had died on January 17, 1801, and suspected she had spent her final weeks in London (Lambeth, Bedfordbury, and Queen Street—all referenced in Mrs. Hunter's journal or in J. Wood's account—are in London). Beyond this I knew very little.

I knew nothing, for instance, about Mr. Hunter—neither

his first name nor how he and Mary Clulow came to marry. I didn't know where the Hunters had lived in London, nor whether they belonged to an Anglican or Methodist church (at the end of the eighteenth century, Methodist meetinghouses, called "chapels," were just beginning to think of themselves as churches in their own right, some more independent than others from the Church of England). I didn't know what Mrs. Hunter looked like, or whether she had any living descendants. I didn't know for a fact whether she had actually had children—whether J. Wood had gotten things right when he referred to her "domestic duties and little ones." I didn't know who J. Wood was, nor how he knew Mary Hunter, nor how he came to have access to Mrs. Hunter's journal.

Before leaving for England, I made contact online with a woman who had done extensive genealogical work on the Clulow family line. She sent me a number of family wills. One of them, it seemed clear to me, had to be that of Mrs. Hunter's father. Written and signed by a John Clulow of Macclesfield, the will was dated November 8, 1789, and made reference to a daughter, Mary, who was not yet twenty-one years old. The math was perfect—the Mary Clulow who would become Mrs. Hunter would have been fifteen years old at the time.

John Clulow wrote his will on long paper in a flowing hand, beginning this way:

> In the Name of the Father Son and holy Ghost three persons but one God Amen—I John Clulow of Macclesfield in the County of Chester, Baker—Being through infinite Mercy in good Bodily health, and of a Perfectly Sound and composed mind, and knowing the certainty of death to my long and wished for home—I

do make this my last will and testament in manner and form following—that is to say first I commit my body to the dust to be buried in the most plain and decent manner at the discretion of my Executors hereafter named. I commend my soul into the hands of Almighty God, my Saviour and Redeemer, in sure and certain hope of a Resurrection to Eternal life through our Lord and Saviour Jesus Christ—And for the settling of my temporal Estate and all such goods and chattels and debts and money as it hath pleased God to bestow upon me, I do give and dispose of the same in the manner and form following.

In his will John Clulow bequeathed to "my daughter Mary" a number of Macclesfield properties, unless "it should please God that my said daughter Mary shall die under the age of twenty one years old and without issue." John Clulow died in 1790, and so in 1795, upon reaching the age of twenty-one, Mary Clulow Hunter had become a wealthy woman.

Further correspondence with my new friend, the genealogist, allowed me to piece together a picture of Mary Clulow's family of origin. Her father, John, had married Elizabeth Whittakers and together they had (at least) five children: William lived from 1757 to 1821; John from 1759 to 1830; Aaron from 1761 to 1795; and Mary from 1775 to 1801. Another girl, Martha, was born and died in 1762. All in all the Clulows had not had bad luck, given what I knew about mortality rates in the late eighteenth century.

While researching the name Clulow, my father found an interesting reference—John Wesley's lawyer was named William Clulow. Surely this must have been Mary's older brother.

When we looked up John Wesley's will, it turned out to have been witnessed on February 25, 1789, by two people—William Clulow and Elizabeth Clulow. The genealogical chart confirmed that William Clulow's wife, like his mother, had been named Elizabeth. What a thrill it must have been for her, I thought, to sign as a witness on John Wesley's will.

Proving himself a more than able research assistant, my father next turned up an interesting reference from an 1840 issue of *The Methodist* magazine:

> James Wood (1751–1840) entered the itineracy in 1773. He exercised an active circuit ministry for fifty years and was twice President of the Wesleyan Conference (1800 and 1808). He settled as a supernumerary in Bristol and at the time of his death at Kingswood was the oldest Methodist preacher in the world.

Surely this was J. Wood—after all, a great many of the accounts published in *The Arminian* had been written by Methodist preachers. Reading J. Wood's obituary, I noted how different the language of Mrs. Hunter's day was from our own—as I had so many times while reading J. Wood's account of Mrs. Hunter's death—and remarked at how adept I had become at deciphering it. An early Methodist preacher was not considered the pastor to a single church; instead he was said to be "itinerant" and was appointed to travel designated preaching "circuits." Neither was he ever considered retired ("once a preacher, always a preacher"); instead he ceased to be counted as eligible for appointment in the annual "conference" of preachers, resulting in his being designated "supernumerated."

J. Wood's status in early Methodism also helped explain

another curiosity: the account of Mrs. Hunter's happy death was longer than almost any other published in *The Arminian*. It made sense that in 1801 the editors would have afforded extra space to the man who had just served as Conference president.

During one week in England, I was able to confirm a great many of my suspicions. In Macclesfield I learned from Tim Brinton, a local historian, that Elizabeth Clulow, Mary's "dear mother," was one of the first parishioners in Macclesfield's St. Michael's Church to be persuaded by Methodist teaching. She was instrumental in launching Christ Church, the "new" Anglican church in town whose "Methodistic" preacher, David Simpson, was one of John Wesley's favorites. (David Simpson had also served as "clerk" in the making of John Clulow's will.)

In Chester, where church archives for the county are stored, I browsed the burial records of Macclesfield churches, looking for deaths of Clulows and Hunters. The Christ Church parish records confirmed John Clulow's burial on November 6, 1790 (he was 56 years old), and Elizabeth Clulow's on January 10, 1793, at the age of 61. Sure enough, her death was "betwixt five and six weeks" after Mary Clulow "found peace" in December 1792. There was no specific sign of Mary Clulow Hunter, though, in the records at Chester.

In Oxford I met with Peter Forsaith, a Methodist historian who helped me to confirm that J. Wood was assigned to London preaching circuits in 1799, 1800, and 1801. He was the author of several instructional pamphlets distributed to Methodist preachers, including one entitled *A Class Book, Containing Directions for Class Leaders*. He was a specialist, of sorts, in organizing people into class meetings, the small accountability groups in which they were encouraged to examine the state of their souls and "work out their own salvation." James Wood's reference to Mrs. Hunter's participation in a class meeting was more than incidental—he had been one of her pastors. He might well have presided at her funeral, and in doing so would have come into possession of her journal.

All of this led me to suspect that Mary Hunter must have been buried—as were thousands of early Methodists—in the yard at Wesley's Chapel, on City Road in London. Few of the graves remain in place at this location—several generations of buildings have covered hundreds of graves, and hundreds more have been relocated across the years. The floor of the Wesley Museum, in the basement of the City Road buildings, in fact consists of smoothed gravestones, their engravings worn away by generations of visitors' feet.

A registry of burials at Wesley's Chapel—the original hand-written entries now transcribed neatly into type—confirmed my suspicion. Entry #1659 looked like this:

1801

Jan 21   Mrs Mary Hunter   26 years   1659   1-1-0
           Marylebone St

The figure 1659 is the number of the burial record. The hyphenated figures referred to the price of the burial—one pound, one shilling, no pence.

"Well, this is where she was buried," I said to the museum staff, who confirmed there was no remaining gravestone. "Who knows? Maybe I'm standing right on top of her." Though I wasn't thinking of it at the time, I am reminded now of Isaac Newton's famous saying that if we hope to see far, it will be by standing on the shoulders of giants.

The next day a friend and I walked the length of Marylebone Street in London. Now a part of London's inner ring, Marylebone was, in the late eighteenth century, one of London's fastest-growing suburbs, and the main street in Marylebone became known as one of the finest in all the city. Reading a little history in the office of the Marylebone Church, I learned that the neighborhood was known in these years for its concentration of Methodists, including Charles Wesley, who was now buried in the churchyard. In the church's sanctuary I found myself imagining Mrs. Hunter sitting in one of the pews, and in the London archives I found the following entry for May 22, 1796, in the baptismal record of the St. Marylebone parish:

> James Hunter, of William and Mary, born April 22, 1796.

This was surely the first of Mary Hunter's "little ones," born about eighteen months after her marriage in August of 1794.

The name William Hunter rang a bell, and once again I was glad my father had come along for the trip. While in Oxford, he had looked up "Hunter" in the index to John Wesley's journal. The single reference was to an Irish family from Glenarm, with whom Wesley stayed while visiting Dublin and its environs in 1771. The footnote to the journal entry noted that the Betty and William Hunter with whom Wesley stayed were the parents of James Hunter, a London surgeon who for over fifty years had "a large practice among the Methodists of

Islington." A quick look at a London A-Z map confirmed that Islington and Marylebone are adjacent boroughs. I just knew that James Hunter, the famous doctor, had to have brothers. Sure enough, one was William, named after his father.

I never did find a record of Mary Clulow's marriage to William Hunter—perhaps they never registered in their Anglican parish, not an uncommon practice for Methodists in those days. But it is not hard for me to imagine how they might have met in London, traveling in the heady circles of the emerging Methodist movement. Perhaps Mary Clulow was visiting her well-connected brother, William. Perhaps William Hunter was visiting his famous brother, James, or perhaps he had moved to London himself. It seems probable that they named their first son James in honor of his highly esteemed uncle.

I do not know what became of James, the son of William and Mary Hunter, nor if he had siblings (we found no other baptismal records). I do not know if James's father William remarried after Mrs. Hunter's happy death, or if the family line survived. Working forward in genealogical work is notoriously difficult, especially when pursuing common surnames. And so my search for Mrs. Hunter concluded without unearthing any physical "treasure." I found no portrait to gaze upon, nor a diary to hold in my hands.

In the end this seemed only fitting, that Mrs. Hunter should elude me still. When I first came across the account of her happy death, sitting in the basement of a seminary library, I was completely captivated by her, in part for the air of secrecy in which she was enveloped. She was like no one I had ever met and yet, at the same time, reminded me of so very many people.

The same feeling came over me while browsing the archives

in Macclesfield—though looking for traces of Mrs. Hunter, I was overwhelmed by the litany of names that sounded familiar to me. Scanning the rolls of the Macclesfield dead, I recognized surname after surname, passed down to people I have known in my work as a parish pastor, people who have proven so faithful in their living and dying. Here are just a few: Orme, Boothe, Davies, Hill, Whitehead, Wright, Metcalf, Thompson, Walter, Moores, Jackson, Owen, Hudson, Clarke, Scott, Lowe, Hall, Hayes, Cooke, Smith, Hatton, Whitaker, Hooper, Warren, Phillips, Marsh, Brown, Williams, Mills, Johnson, Ridgway, Faulkner, Atkinson, Mellor, Johnson, Bullock, Dawson, Crowder, Grubb, Turner, Brooks, Wilson, Higgins, Rose, Taylor, Armstrong, Delany.

Whether or not Mrs. Hunter has biological descendants, she has spiritual descendants galore. I count myself among them.

APPENDIX

"An Account of Mrs. Hunter's Holy Life and Happy Death" by J. Wood

[Wood's account was published in the July and August 1801 editions of *The Arminian* magazine. I have indicated references to Part One chapter titles and Part Two "lessons" in brackets.]

Whatever degree of Grace is communicated by the Lord Jesus Christ, the Head of the Church, to any individual, is not intended for the good of that person only, but that he might shine as a light in the family, the church and the world [Chapter 1]. Hence it becomes a duty in the receiver to communicate to his Christian friends, while he is able to attend to the worship of God; and when deprived of this privilege, to shine in a suffering state [Chapter 2].

The light of truth and holiness appearing in the last stage of life should be carefully collected for the good of surviving relatives, and, when proper, handed down to posterity [Chapter 3]. With this view I shall endeavour to give as faithful an account of Mrs. Hunter, as possible; and I shall have the less difficulty in this as she left in her own hand writing some information respecting her conversion, her sorrows, and consolations. I shall, therefore, have little more to do than transcribe from her own papers, except here and there to add a few words by way of elucidation.

Mrs. Hunter was the daughter of the late Mr. Clulow, of Macclesfield. Her very pious and excellent mother was peculiarly attentive to her education, and laboured early in life to point out the way of salvation to her. This parental care was crowned with the divine blessing; the Lord, by a variety of means, drew her to himself, as appears from her own account [Chapter 4].

> Of a truth, I am a child of many mercies: The Lord often alarmed my conscience by representing unto me in dreams, the dissolution of the world; and attracted my heart by affording me happy sensations of his goodness when I was but a child; tho' I could not then conceive from whence this happiness came, nor how it went. I always felt uncomfortable, when these divine influences were withdrawn. When about seven years of age, I frequently got *Janeway's Token for Children*, went into a room, and read it by myself: I then prayed that God would make me as happy as those little children of whom I had read, and as sure of going to heaven as they were [Chapter 5]. One time when I had been reading and praying

over that little book, as I was coming out of the room it was impressed on my mind to turn back and pray again. I thought I have prayed once, that is enough, and took hold of the door to come out; but the impression to return and pray again, was so strong that I obeyed the call, and was filled with such happiness that I thought, if I then died, I was sure of going to heaven.

From that time till she was about twelve years of age, she had many drawings from God, but no deep work upon her mind. At that time she joined the Methodist Society, at Macclesfield, and in her outward conduct was blameless; yet she evidently continued to *seek* only, without *striving* to enter in at the strait gate. When about fifteen years old, she had some symptoms of a decline, but recovered her health and increased in strength. What follows is her own account of her finding peace.

When I was about eighteen years and four months old, I saw clearly, that unless my sins were forgiven me, I could not go to heaven. I then began to seek the Lord with my whole heart [Chapter 6]. For one month I was in deep distress, but at length proved the faithful promise verified, "Ye shall seek me, and find me, when ye shall search for me with all your heart." On a Friday, in Dec. 1792, Mr. Shadford preached in Macclesfield, from these words, "Fear not, little flock; for it is your Father's good pleasure to give you the kingdom." While sitting under that sermon, the Lord condescended to give my distressed soul a power to believe that I was gathered into that little flock. My distress abated, but I had not

APPENDIX

much joy that night. The next day, my whole heart engaged in prayer: I ventured to say, "I believe that Jesus died to save my soul, and if I perish, I will still believe that he died for me." The Lord removed my guilt and sorrow, gave me the witness of his Spirit, and filled my soul with peace and joy.

Betwixt five and six weeks after I found peace, the Lord was pleased to take my dear mother to himself. Before her death she looked at me, and said,—"I am going to leave thee, Mary, in a troublesome world, fatherless and motherless; but I leave thee in the hands of God" [Chapter 7]. After her death, I was led much to view the goodness of my heavenly Father, who had condescended to be my Support and Refuge thro' the trial. I was so exceedingly happy in the Lord, that I even longed to die. When my dear mother was in her coffin, I went several times into the room alone, and from my heart repeated,

Ah, lovely appearance of death, &c. [Chapter 8]

The night after she was buried, I was so supported by the Lord, and convinced that He did all things well, that I was enabled to say,—"The Lord gave, and the Lord hath taken away; blessed be the name of the Lord." For many days these words were continually running through my mind with great sweetness,

There is my house, my portion fair;
My treasure and my heart are there,
And my abiding home!

Not long after the death of her mother, she was led to see and feel her want of a greater change from sin to holiness [Chapter 9]. In speaking on this subject, she says, "These words came into my mind,—'Without holiness, no man shall see the Lord.' I was then happy, but prayed that God would make me holy. The more I prayed, the more I saw the necessity of purity of heart. I knew that God, for Christ's sake, had forgiven all my sins; yet I could not rest in that enjoyment alone."

From this time, for about a fortnight, she was much in the exercise of prayer, continuing three hours together in a morning on her knees, pleading with the Lord for the accomplishment of his precious promises [Lesson #1]. In one of the seasons of retirement, while agonizing with the Lord in prayer for that perfect love which casteth out all fear that hath torment, the desire of her soul was fulfilled, which she describes as follows.

> One Tuesday morning, about 7 o'clock, while on my knees, these words came to my mind,—"I will; be thou clean." The enemy suggested, that they were not for me; I said to the Lord, "surely they are for me: This is what I want, and am seeking." These words were repeatedly applied with power to my soul; and altho' the enemy strove to embarrass me with his suggestions, yet I resolved to keep them in my memory by repeating them [Lesson #2]. I rose from my knees, and soon after opened the Bible, and cast my eyes on these words,—"Thou shalt be holy; for the Lord thy God is holy." I was filled with such a degree of tranquility, that wherever I turned, all was calm; my peace flowed as a river; Glory and thanks

be to my God. A circumstance occurred a few days after, which more fully satisfied me, that the Lord had wrought a great change in my heart;—I was sitting in my room, when the servant came running in and said, "O dear Miss Clulow, somebody has been throwing at your bedroom window, and smashed all the window in." I sat calm and unmoved, and felt no more resentment against the person, than if he had done me a kindness.

In the Spring following she was much indisposed, but was very happy, as will appear from her own words:

> After I was turned nineteen, I got well in body, and retained my spiritual health. Soon after I went to Congleton, where, a person hearing of my experience, said, "Ah, Miss Clulow is on the mount now, but she will soon be in the valley like other people." This saying came to my ears; but instead of its being any discouragement to me, it was like a spur to drive me nearer to the Lord by watchfulness and prayer: I had such a holy fear of losing my confidence, that for several months I prayed twenty times a day, besides lifting up my heart, when my hands were employed in my domestic duties. Very frequently when I went into any room in the house where I could not be seen, I dropped on my knees, and prayed for strength to hold fast the beginning of my confidence to the end, and that I might never become lukewarm. Thanks be to my God, he breathed into my heart an ardent desire, which nothing but the constant enjoyment of his favour could satisfy. Thro' divine grace, in the exercise of visiting the sick and praying

with them; and taking up my cross daily, I have been a conqueror, and not a captive [Lesson #3]. When any persons strive to do me any injury, instead of feeling anger, I feel pity and love to their souls, and rejoice when an opportunity offers, to return to them a kindness. And when any remarkably trying circumstance has occurred, I have been led to entreat the Lord to save me in the trial, from grieving his Holy Spirit, and to proportion my strength to my day; and by using the grace bestowed upon me, and supplicating for more, I have been kept in the trial. O, may sincere gratitude flow from my heart, and may I ever please and glorify my indulgent, my heavenly Father: He has been faithful to me and brought me thro' the slippery paths of youth, and settled me in life beyond my expectation.

As Mrs. Hunter occasionally wrote the state of her mind for some years before her death, tho' she kept no regular diary, what follows will be chiefly taken from those accounts, till the time of her last sickness.

June 21, 1795 . . . This being my birthday, I was much led out in sweet reflection on the past year [Lesson #4]. I find a growth in grace, and in the knowledge and love of God; more readiness to suffer his will, and patience in bearing when falsely accused.

June 23. This morning my mind was much refreshed in reading of the children of Israel, when Pharaoh with all his host pursued them; they cried to the Lord and were delivered. When troubles pursue, and the enemy tempts

to doubt of the favour of God, O my soul! fly to Jesus
thy Mediator,—

> *Who ever lives for thee to pray*
> *And cannot pray in vain.*

He partook of our flesh and blood, and suffered,
being tempted, that he might be a merciful and faithful
High Priest, and able to succour them that are tempted.
When my consolations are at a low ebb, and my way
is cloudy, if the powers of darkness pursue me, as the
Egyptians did the children of Israel; fear not, O my
soul, but stand still, and see the salvation of God. He
will again visit me, and shine with double luster, and my
peace will flow like a river. Thanks be to God, that he
hath revealed this salvation to me a worm!—

> *I the chief of sinners am,*
> *But Jesus died for me.*

I enjoy sweet communion and fellowship with God,
and it is the earnest desire of my soul to be kept from
saying, doing, or even thinking any thing that would offend him [Lesson #5]. O my Lord, cleanse the thoughts
of my heart by the inspiration of the Holy Spirit.
"Cleanse,—and keep me clean."

June 25. I feel my soul much alive to God. Sometimes,
when I am sitting under the precious Word, I drink of
the celestial Streams, which flow from the Fountain of
Life [Lesson #6]. If what I now feel is but a drop from

the unexhausted Ocean of eternal Bliss, O when I reach
my Mansion above, my capacious soul shall drink its
fill,

> *Where faith is sweetly lost in sight,*
> *And hope in full, supreme delight,*
> *And everlasting love.*

There I shall have angels and saints for my companions, be with God my Father and Jesus my Friend, my
Saviour, my all in all. O my God! While my spirit is
confined in this house of clay, be thou my Keeper and
my Guide, until thou hast made me fully meet to be
gathered into eternal rest!

While I have been writing, the enemy has been trying to discourage me; but, thro' divine assistance, thanks
be to God, he put me in remembrance, that all things
are possible with him. May I be enabled to hold fast
whereunto I have attained. I do in real sincerity, long to
be filled with the Holy Spirit; to be influenced by him in
every thought, word, and action, that I may truly please
and glorify thee, O my God.

From this time Mrs. Hunter, by some means omitted writing down what she felt in her mind for several years. Whether
this omission was occasioned by attention to her little ones and
other domestic duties; by her concern for the sick and dying,
or any other engagement, is not easy to determine; but there is
good reason to hope that it was not from any loss she had suffered in her Christian experience. During these years of silence
her leisure time was partly employed in visiting the Sick-Ward

in one of the Workhouses, where she regularly attended once or twice a week, talking to the poor women and praying with them, till nearly exhausted. Her labour of love in this way was crowned with the divine blessing [Lesson #7]. Some of those who trifled away health and strength, in ignorance and folly, were brought to cry for mercy, and were indeed as brands plucked out of the fire. Some persons thought she went too far in going from one to another in the ward, and praying with divers persons one after another, some of whom were nearly deaf and could hear nothing except when she was very near them, and others were labouring under very contagious fevers, yet nothing that was said, could ever induce her to shun the cross, or leave those poor creatures in their ignorance, to die without warning. This part of her life yielded her the greatest satisfaction a little before her last illness.

Having been useful to some persons in the sick-ward, who recovered from their affliction, that they might be assisted to hold fast the good which they had gained, she met once a week as a class; and though some of them through age died and went to heaven, yet the number increased, and at the time when she was taken ill, there were about twenty of them. These poor young women were so much affected with the news of her death, that they could scarcely have felt more if they had lost the most tender and affectionate parent. May many members of our Society, copy her example, and exceed her in usefulness.

> *Jan. 1, 1799* . . . For ever blessed be my heavenly Father, at this hour, the first of the new year, I feel Jesus is mine, my Saviour, my friend, my all in all. I am united to him, I trust by inseparable ties. I derive virtue from

him and feel the life his wounds impart. My soul truly delights in God. I have no other hope, nor wish to have any other plea for present and eternal salvation, but that my precious Jesus lived and died for me. It is now a little more than six years since I found the name of Jesus like ointment poured forth: it was truly the very balm my wounded soul stood in need of. Oh that I may never forget his benefits; but may all the powers of my soul praise and magnify thee, O my God, my eternal portion. I shall dwell with thee thro' all eternity. A few more sufferings, and I shall rest in thine embrace. Glory be to God and the Lamb forever.

March 11. My precious Jesus was crucified as an expiatory sacrifice, and by his stripes are we healed: He purchased our justification and sanctification. Humbly depending on God every moment for fresh supplies of strength, and all we need for time and eternity, is, I believe, acceptable to God.

[*March*] 26. I feel, "I nothing am;—I nothing have," of myself; but Christ is my all: He is my Rock, my Refuge, my Strength. Glory be to God, while my hands are employed in domestic duties, my heart is sweetly engaged with him who is my supreme delight. My soul feeds on heavenly manna, and longs to be with him whom I love.

[*March*] 28. Glory be to God, that amidst friends and reputation, health and plenty;—He is the only source of all my joy. In him my soul fixes all her hopes. I rest in celestial calm. O help me still to flee from the world, and live to thee alone!

[*March*] 29. Thou, O my God, condescendest to bless me in my going out, and coming in; in my basket, and in my store: thy blessing will go before me as a light, and follow as my protecting angel: When I lay down it will defend me, and I shall rest safely in the arms of my Beloved. When trials and temptations raise a storm, thou canst bid my soul be still; and all shall obey thee. I depend only on thee: Thou art a sufficient and a never-failing helper. When thou smilest, all the world may frown. Thou art the chief object of my fear, and all my desires are directed to thee.

In the following month, . . . as Mrs. Hunter was going to a prayer-meeting, at Queen-Street, she saw a young woman who was apparently in great want. Mrs. H. advised her to go into the workhouse; the poor creature said, she had an aged mother to support, and was come out that morning to beg something for her. As such accounts in London are numerous, and most of them fallacious, her story was not believed; but Mrs. H. felt uneasy in her mind, and thought, if it should be true, it was a pity the aged woman should die of want. She, therefore, after meeting, went in search of the poor woman, and, after much fruitless enquiry, at length found her and her poor daughter in a garret: the mother was eighty-two years of age, happy in God, and waiting for her blessed change from the pains and sorrows of mortality, to the unmixed joys of the heavenly society.

I mention this circumstance for two reasons: I. To shew,

that the accounts of woe, which we hear, even in London, are not all feigned: And 2. that there may be found some instances of sterling piety in obscure garrets or cellars, labouring under the accumulated burthen of poverty, pain, and comparative neglect.

> *April 16.* I have frequently found that before trials and temptations came, I have been remarkably drawn out in prayer, that my heavenly Father would make perfect his strength in my weakness; and the recollection of this has enabled me to look up for help. O that he may supply what is lacking!

> *[April]* 29. O the love of Christ! How sweet a banquet! I feel the life which shall never end. He that walketh uprightly, walketh surely! O God strengthen me to do always the things that please thee. By grace I am saved. Jesus is my righteousness. I offer myself and all I do, to him. My soul longs for a fuller union with God; more faith and love! O the delight, the happiness I feel! A stranger intermeddleth not with it. O for more of this uninterrupted tranquility of soul! I have, as yet, but a drop from the ocean of eternal happiness.

> *A point my good, a drop my store,*
> *Eager I ask, I pant for more.*

> O how sweet it is to retire from the world; yea, even from the company of pious Christians, when profitable, spiritual conversation seems to be ended.

June 21. This morning, while reading Henry's Notes on the 17th chapter of John, my heavenly Father gave me to see what I have long wished to know, the way how I might glorify him. He pitied my ignorance, and supplied my want. I am but a child, a dwarf, in religion. I immediately kneeled down to thank him and entreat that if I was wrong, he would direct me. It came sweetly to my mind, "This is the way: walk thou in it."

July 23. I found my heart singularly drawn out in fervent prayer, that God would, from that very hour, entirely remove out of my nature every inclination to expose the faults of others, or to hear persons speak against anyone.

[July] 29. O for more heavenly wisdom and spiritual understanding, to discern between what is only temptation, and what is sin! Thou dost, O heavenly Father, in the time of trial, give me power to look to thee for strength; yet in some conflicts, I am but *just accepted.*

Aug. 2. I have learned to live the present moment by faith, and am saved by grace [Lesson #8]. O create in me more sincere gratitude and love to thee, my heavenly Father, for thine unbounded love to me thy poor child.

[Aug.] 8. This is my wedding day. I have been married five years. For ever praised be my heavenly Father, he has been far better to me than all my fears. My great concern, before I was married, was, lest, when I should have a young family, I should grow dead to God; but thanks be to him, he has given me to prove his grace sufficient

to keep my soul alive to him in all situations. I now see it was his love to me that he planted those fears in my heart, to drive me nearer to himself. Glory be to God, I have been going forward ever since I was married. My soul is considerably established in grace, in faith, knowledge, and love, and in a filial fear of grieving my God.

Sept. 3. Glory, honour and praise, be to my compassionate God! He hath condescended to hear the sincere breathings of my soul. After private prayer, as I was coming down stairs in sweet tranquility of mind, the still small voice gently whispered, "Thou art my love, my fair one; there is no spot in thee!" Returning again to my room, almost immediately after I kneeled down, it was brought to my mind, "Thou art made whole: watch and pray lest thou again fall into temptation." My Lord and my God! The desire of my heart is that I may from this moment prove, by happy experience, that I am thoroughly renewed in all the powers and faculties of my soul: that I may be thine entirely, growing up into thee my living Head in all things. Thou hast this morning brought me one step higher up the heavenly ladder; O give me full proof that I am established and fixed firm, never to go back.

Oct. 4. Although poorly in body, I enjoy health of soul: though in the world, yet, through divine grace, I am not of the world. Glory be to my God, the sincere breathing of my heart is, that my body may be a temple for the Holy Spirit to dwell in, while I am absent from the regions above. When Jesus shall take me to himself, I shall behold his glory, and dwell for ever with him.

[Oct.] 31. My soul lives in the happy enjoyment of God. Jesus is mine, and I am his. I love him, and he loves me:—

> *O may we never parted be,*
> *'Till I become one spirit with thee.*

Dec. 4. Glory be to God, I see more and more into my ignorance, weakness, and helplessness; but the Lord is my teacher: He is my strength, my all in all. O that I may ever see myself in his own light, and feel a momentary dependence on him!

Dec. 21. I see and feel the necessity of that atonement Jesus hath made for me.

> *This all my hope, and all my plea,*
> *Jesus hath liv'd, hath died for me.*

My soul rejoices in Christ, and has no confidence in the flesh. I feel thankful for the grace which I enjoy: I live by faith, and all my salvation is of God; it is he that giveth me inclination and ability to think and do what is well-pleasing to him. By obeying his Spirit, I find he leads me on to more light, life and love. Glory to God!

Much larger extracts might have been made from Mrs. Hunter's memorandums: but on account of the sameness of ideas and expressions, which is common in such writings, I have laboured to be sparing herein, especially as she had not the most happy way of expressing her thoughts with her pen.

It was remarked by several of Mrs. Hunter's most intimate

friends, for some time before her illness, that her growth in grace was considerable, that she was visibly ripening for the heavenly garner: a much greater deadness to the world, and more heavenly-mindedness, appeared in her on all occasions when she was in their company. And it seems probable, that she had some presentiment of her approaching dissolution, for just before she was taken ill, she said to an intimate friend, "I cannot account for it, but I had an impression on my mind, when at Bedfordbury prayer-meeting, that I had something to do, which I have now done; and it seems that I have now nothing more to do on earth."

The last Sunday in the year 1800, Mrs. H. attended a Lovefeast at Lambeth, where she bore her testimony to the goodness and power of God in cleansing from all unrighteousness, and keeping those who cleave to him in perfect peace, and stedfast hope of unclouded glory [Lesson #9]. At the request of the person who kept the Love-fest, she prayed with peculiar fervor: the influence of the Holy Spirit was eminently on the congregation, which made it a time of refreshing from the presence of the Lord. About nine days after, she was taken ill of a putrid fever, which very soon brought on a delirium, accompanied with great depression of spirit; yet she had some intervals of recollection, and in all those seasons was happy in God. In one of these a friend asked her if Christ was precious? To whom she answered,—"Yes, very precious: he supports my soul in such a manner, that it is heaven on earth to be afflicted. I have no wish to live or die: I am in God's hands; let him do what seemeth him good. I had a sore conflict with the enemy yesterday, but the Lord set my soul at liberty, with these words:

To patient faith the prize is sure;—
And all that to the end endure
The cross, shall wear the crown.

" 'Fear not, for I am with thee. Behold, I go to prepare a place for thee, that where I am, thou mayest be also' [Lesson #10]. What a precious Saviour is Christ to my soul! Away with all beside; away with it. What could I do now, if I had not this Saviour?" When asked if she thought her sickness would be unto death, she answered—"I know not: I have not an anxious thought about it; I only desire that God may support me through life and death."

A week before her departure, when the same friend said to her,—"I hope you continue stedfast?"—she replied, "I know not: for the enemy tempts me in such a manner that I seem to be bewildered." She requested her friend to pray for her, that God would give her strength, and support her to the last. From this time she was seldom sensible for many minutes together till near her end; but it appeared from her expressions that Satan, the cruel adversary of men, laboured by suggestions and accusations to wrest from her the shield of faith, and make her passage through the valley of the shadow of death, as painful as possible.

The night before she died, between eleven and twelve o'clock, she sang with a loud voice, "Hallelujah, Hallelujah, Hallelujah." About one o'clock she said to the young person who sat up with the nurse, "The enemy has deceived me long enough; but he shall deceive me no more: he shall not have me. O what a deliverance! What great grace!" Nearly two hours after, she exclaimed aloud,—"The carriage is come! The carriage is come for me! O what a beautiful carriage! It is come for me; and I am coming; I am coming! O how clear the way is! I shall soon be there. Glory! Glory! Glory! O what great grace! Angels are come for me! Cannot you see them? Bless the Lord! Bless the Lord!" Then turning her face to the pillow, she said,—"O how easy! How easy!" From that time she spoke no more to be understood; but lay from three, till about seven o'clock, when she took her happy flight to the joys of the Lord, on Saturday, Jan. 17, 1801.

Thus died Mrs. Hunter, in the prime of life, (about 26 years of age,) and in the prospect of great usefulness. Her soul was bent on doing good, and her leisure time was employed in visiting the sick and needy. Mr. Hunter assured me, that during the years he was married to her, he had never seen a temper, nor heard a word from her, inconsistent with the Christian Character. May God raise up many more such examples of pure and undefiled religion.

London, May 4, 1801
J. Wood

CHAPTER NOTES

Meeting Mrs. Hunter for the First Time

The library in which I found archives of *The Arminian* was at the Claremont School of Theology (Claremont, California). Professor Ann Taves and the students in her graduate seminar on religious practices were instrumental in helping me see the happy death as a ritualized expression of religious faith as practiced in early modern England.

For more on religious rituals and their transmission, see the extensive literature on the theory of religious practice, much of which has been published in the past generation in response to Pierre Bourdieu's *Outline of a Theory of Practice* (Cambridge: Cambridge University Press, 1977).

Part One

CHAPTER 1: WHATEVER DEGREE OF GRACE:
SHARING GOD'S GREATEST GIFT

David Stannard's *The Puritan Way of Death* (New York: Oxford University Press, 1977) was extraordinarily helpful to me in mapping the changes in the theory and practice of dying across the fifteenth, sixteenth, and seventeenth centuries.

Jacques Barzun's magisterial *From Dawn to Decadence* (New York: HarperCollins, 2000) helped me see connections between the practices of dying and the larger currents of intellectual and cultural life in Europe.

Among dozens of works about the Wesley brothers, I found especially helpful John Tyson's edited volume, *Charles Wesley: A Reader* (Oxford: Oxford University Press, 1989).

George Regas is the Rector Emeritus of All Saints' Episcopal Cathedral in Pasadena, California.

CHAPTER 2: TO SHINE IN A SUFFERING STATE:
THIS LITTLE LIGHT OF MINE

All Bible quotations in this book are from the King James Version. For a lively and informative history of the KJV and its lasting influence in shaping the language and culture of England and America, see Adam Nicolson's *God's Secretaries: The Making of the King James Bible* (New York: HarperCollins, 2003).

For remarkable accounts of some of the early Christian martyrs, see *The Acts of the Christian Martyrs*, edited and translated by Herbert Musurillo (Oxford: Clarendon Press, 1972). Thanks to Professor Greg Riley of the Claremont Graduate University for this lead.

Chapter 3: Handed Down to Posterity: The Life of a Story

The Arminian was first published in London in 1778. In 1798 the editors officially changed the publication's name to *The Methodist*. The original title (*The Arminian*) continued to be printed on the magazine's cover in parentheses, however, and readers continued to refer to the magazine in this way well into the nineteenth century. J. Wood's account of Mrs. Hunter's happy death is entirely representative of the deathbed narratives that were published across this time span, though over the course of the nineteenth century the accounts became shorter and more likely to focus on the lives and deaths of preachers and other notable Methodists rather than "ordinary" laypeople.

The historian A. Gregory Schneider has written on the early Methodists' practice of the happy death: "The Ritual of Happy Dying among Early American Methodists" (*Church History* 56:3, September 1987).

Chapter 4: Crowned with the Divine Blessing: The Paradox of Death

I found the prayer for a happy death in *Daily Prayers* (Sacred Heart Monastery, Hales Corners, WI).

The association of Joseph and a "happy death" dates at least to the early seventeenth century, when the story of Joseph's death was included in *The Mystical City of God*, a four-volume history of the life of the Blessed Virgin Mary, created by Venerable Mother Mary of Jesus of Agreda, a Spanish nun.

Perhaps more familiar to recent generations of Catholics will be the "Prayer for a Happy Death," written by John Henry Cardinal Newman in the nineteenth century, to which Pope

Pius X attached the following indulgence in 1846: "O My Lord and Saviour, support me in my last hour by the strong arms of Thy Sacraments and the fragrance of Thy consolations. Let Thy absolving words be said over me, and the holy oil sign and seal me; and let Thine own body be my food, and Thy Blood my sprinkling; and let Thy Mother Mary come to me, and my Angel whisper peace to me, and Thy glorious saints and my own dear patrons smile on me; that, in and through them all, I may die as I desire to live, in Thy Church, in Thy Faith, and in Thy Love. Amen."

Chapter 5: Sure of Going to Heaven: Love Like an Ocean

I struggled to summarize in a few short paragraphs the great doctrinal struggle between Calvinism and Arminianism. Ward McAfee, Professor of History, Emeritus, at California State University San Bernardino, helped greatly with a critique of one of my earliest drafts. I also found Robert C. Monk's *John Wesley: His Puritan Heritage* (Lanham, MD: Scarecrow Press, 1999) helpful as I boiled things down.

Because Calvinists have, for the most part, written the most popular versions of early American history, the influence of Methodism (and Arminianist theology) in the shaping of American culture is just now beginning to be appreciated. See, for instance, Katherine Long's article "The Power of Interpretation: The Revival of 1857–1858 and the Historiography of Revivalism in America," in *Religion and American Culture* 4:1 (Winter 1994).

A recent Swedish study of almost five hundred parents of dying children shows the merits of addressing issues of death and dying with children directly. According to the study,

"None of the 147 parents who talked with their child about death regretted it. In contrast, 69 of 258 parents (27 percent) who did not talk with their child about death regretted not having done so." ("Talking About Death with Children Who Have Severe Malignant Disease" by Ulrika Kreicbergs et al., *New England Journal of Medicine* 351:12, September 16, 2004).

The baptismal liturgy I used with Jason Robb is the one found in the *United Methodist Hymnal* (Nashville: United Methodist Publishing House, 1989).

As is the case with so many other jewels, I found the excerpts from the Puritan alphabet and the quote from the Anne Bradstreet poem in Stannard's *The Puritan Way of Death*.

CHAPTER 6: THE WHOLE HEART: ON EARTH AS IT IS IN HEAVEN

Especially in his latter years, John Wesley liked to argue that for his doctrine on holiness he had merely drawn on some of the most familiar classics from the shelf of Puritan literature: Thomas à Kempis's *Imitation of Christ* (written in the early fifteenth century, the work was distributed widely in England during the sixteenth and seventeenth centuries), Jeremy Taylor's *Holy Living* (1650) and *Holy Dying* (1651), and William Law's *A Practical Treatise on Christian Perfection* (1726) and *Serious Call to a Devout and Holy Life* (1729). See Samuel Rogal's *John and Charles Wesley* (Boston: Twayne Publishers, 1983). The reality, of course, was that Wesley and other proponents of holiness in the eighteenth century, while indeed tapping a historic stream within the Christian tradition, were giving it a distinctive flavor and emphasis. Wesley's mix of historic Christian theology and modern aspiration had great appeal for people seeking to exercise their own spiritual muscles. Propelled by a well-organized cadre of itinerant preachers, Methodism became the fastest-growing religious movement in England and America from the mid-eighteenth to the late nineteenth century.

CHAPTER 7: IN THE HANDS OF GOD: *Entre Tus Manos, Señor*

In the biblically shaped view of those living at the turn of the nineteenth century, the entire cosmos is possessed by God. In the words of the psalmist:

> Whither shall I go from thy spirit? or whither shall I flee from thy presence? If I ascend up into heaven, thou art there: if I make my bed in hell, behold, thou art there. If I take the wings of the morning, and dwell in the uttermost parts of the sea; Even there shall thy hand lead me, and thy right hand shall hold me. (Psalm 139:1–3)

CHAPTER 8: AH, LOVELY APPEARANCE OF DEATH: A DOORWAY OPENED ONTO GOD

My thanks to Kimberly Wilton and family for permission to quote from Edith Powell's letters and poems.

CHAPTER 9: A GREATER CHANGE: IN SEARCH OF GOD'S WILL

In his edited volume of Charles Wesley's works (mentioned earlier), John Tyson does a good job of diagnosing the difference between the Wesley brothers over the doctrine of Christian perfection. Charles held that this kind of perfection amounted to the removal of the "stain" of original sin and the consequent restoration in the individual of the *imago dei*, the very image of God. John held that the kind of perfection Charles aspired to could not be attained until *after* death. John preferred to interpret the word through the prism of its usage in the original language of the New Testament, Greek. The word *teleois* in Greek—derived from *telos*, meaning end or final goal—did not mean "flawless," but rather "completed," "mature," or "full grown." The brothers appear to have agreed to disagree about the matter.

For more from Dorothy Bass on religious practice, see her book *Practicing Our Faith* (San Francisco: Jossey-Bass, 1997) or the University of North Carolina website: http://www.unc.edu/depts/practice/definitions.html.

Part Two

Part Two includes thoughts and insights compiled across my fifteen years of pastoral work in local churches, during which the task of weekly preaching has led me to read widely and across disciplines. My intellectual and pastoral debts are too many to name.

Lesson #1: The Exercise of Prayer: Working Out Your Own Salvation

The prayer card I use, compiled by Arden Mead, is published by Creative Communications for the Parish (Fenton, MO).

Lesson #2: Keep the Word: Making the Bible's Story Your Own

Thomas Oden's introduction to *Ancient Christian Commentary on Scripture* is available for download at http://ivpress.gospelcom.net/accs/volumes_and_editors.php.

Lesson #3: Take Up the Cross: Conquering All Things

In writing this chapter I drew heavily on A. Gregory Schneider's *The Way of the Cross Leads Home: The Domestication of*

American Methodism (Bloomington: Indiana University Press, 1993).

Rising above the physical pain of dying was a particular pre-occupation of Charles Wesley, who was almost always sick, it seems, and believed himself throughout his life to be near the edge of death. Wesley popularized an entire genre of hymns, which he published in two volumes entitled "Hymns on the Preparation for Death." Here are a few verses from just one of the hundreds, perhaps thousands, of such hymns he wrote:

> *Come on, my partners in distress,*
> *My comrades through the wilderness,*
> *Who still your bodies feel;*
> *Awhile forget your griefs and fears,*
> *And look beyond this vale of tears,*
> *To that celestial hill . . .*
>
> *Who suffer with our Master here,*
> *We shall before his face appear,*
> *And by his side sit down;*
> *To patient faith the prize is sure,*
> *And all that to the end endure*
> *The cross, shall wear the crown . . .*
>
> *In hope of that ecstatic pause,*
> *Jesus, we now sustain the cross,*
> *And at thy footstool fall;*
> *Till thou our hidden life reveal,*
> *Till thou our ravished spirits fill,*
> *And God is all in all!*

LESSON #4: SWEET REFLECTION ON THE PAST:
RECOGNIZING THE PRESENCE OF GOD

This version of the Examen of Consciousness and the quotation from Cowan and Futrell are found in *Love: A Guide for Prayer* (Winona, MN: Saint Mary's Press, 1985), a prayer book created by Jacqueline Syrup Bergan and Sister Marie Schwan of the Center for Christian Renewal in Crookston, Minnesota.

LESSON #5: ENJOY SWEET COMMUNION:
REMEMBERING THE SAINTS

The liturgy for All Saints Sunday is found in *The United Methodist Book of Worship* (Nashville: United Methodist Publishing House, 1992).

LESSON #6: DRINK FROM THE CELESTIAL STREAM:
SHOUTING OUT YOUR JOY

The historian Lester Ruth chose Garretson's expression as the title to his book about the early American Methodists' "quarterly meetings." See Lester Ruth's *A Little Heaven Below* (Nashville: Abingdon, 2000).

For a fantastic discussion of how Africans and Europeans blended cultures and modes of worship, see Mechal Sobel's *The World They Made Together: Black and White Values in Eighteenth-Century Virginia* (Princeton: Princeton University Press, 1988).

The best discussion of ecstatic religious expression in early modern England and America is Ann Taves's *Fits, Trances and Visions: Experiencing Religion and Explaining Experience from Wesley to James* (Princeton, NJ: Princeton University Press, 1999).

LESSON #7: THE LABOR OF LOVE: LOVING GOD AND NEIGHBOR

I found the quotation from Thomas Merton at: http://www.cin.org/saints/jcross-merton.html.

LESSON #8: LIVE THE PRESENT MOMENT: SEIZING THE DAY

Though I didn't quote it directly, Dorothy Bass's *Receiving the Day: Christian Practices for Opening the Gift of Time* (San Francisco: Jossey-Bass, 1999) served as a nice backdrop to this chapter.

LESSON #9: BEAR TESTIMONY: SHARING A GOOD WORD

The Robert Pretzlaff quote is drawn from his article "At a Loss for Words" in *The Pharos*, Autumn 2004.

For an excellent discussion of end-of-life dilemmas, see "Dying and Decision-Making—Evolution of End-of-Life Options," by Timothy E. Quill, M.D., in *The New England Journal of Medicine* 350:20 (May 13, 2004).

THE PROSPECT OF GREAT USEFULNESS

The question "How well can I die?" combines the title of Ira Byock's *Dying Well* (New York: Riverhead, 1997) with that of Sherwin Nuland's *How We Die* (New York: Vintage, 1992).

For a discussion of projected increases in longevity, and the implications thereof, see Alexander Capron's article "Ethical Aspects of Major Increase in Life Span and Life Expectancy" in Henry J. Aaron and William B. Schwartz's edited volume *Coping with Methusela: The Impact of Molecular Biology on Medicine and Society* (Washington, DC: Brookings Institution Press, 2004). Capron acknowledges ethical distinctions between futures of "prolonged health," "prolonged decline," and "prolonged dying." He does not, though, consider the ethical distinctions that can be drawn between different kinds, or qualities, of death.

EPILOGUE: MEETING MRS. HUNTER AGAIN

It is possible, of course, that Mary Clulow and William Hunter were married in her hometown, Macclesfield. My father and I looked in the marriage records of the Christ Church and St. Michael's parishes in Macclesfield, and the St. Marylebone and Islington parishes of London. We failed to look in the records for Prestbury, the "ancient parish" of Chester County, where between 1754 and 1837 people were required to marry under the Hardwick Marriage Act. Still, many Church of England "dissenters" were getting married outside the church in the second half of the eighteenth century, so much so, in fact, that Parliament passed the Hardwick Marriage Act, requiring marriages to be performed in the Church of England's ancient parishes, staffed by the clergy most loyal to the Crown. Having decided that too many people were marrying outside the church ("jumping the broomstick," etc.), Parliament passed the act in hopes of reining in the marriage practices of those belonging to "dissenting" and "nonconforming" church "sects." My guess is that Mary Clulow and Mary Hunter, devout Methodists, did not subject themselves to a formal, Anglican wedding at Prestbury.

A native of San Diego, John Fanestil is a graduate of Dartmouth College, Oxford University—where he studied as a Rhodes Scholar—and the Claremont School of Theology. Since 1992, Fanestil has been working as a pastor at United Methodist churches in southern California. His writing has appeared in the *Guardian* (London), the *San Diego Union-Tribune*, and the *Los Angeles Times*. *Mrs. Hunter's Happy Death* is his first book.